D0436553

SCENES
FROM
COUNTRY
LIFE ❧

BOOKS BY MALISSA REDFIELD:

The Country of Love
Games of Chance with Strangers
Scenes from Country Life

SCENES FROM COUNTRY LIFE

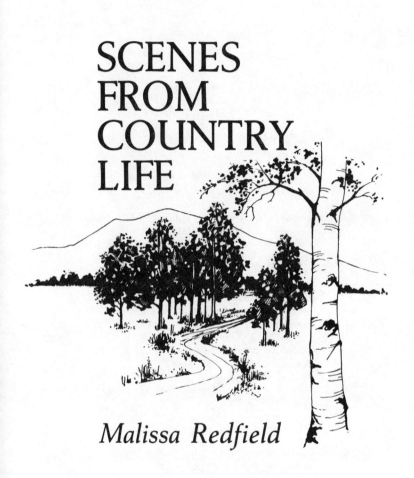

Malissa Redfield

PRENTICE-HALL, INC.,
Englewood Cliffs, N.J.

Book Designer and Illustrator: Linda Huber
Art Director: Hal Siegel

Printed in the United States of America
Prentice-Hall International, Inc., London
Prentice-Hall of Australia, Pty. Ltd., Sydney
Prentice-Hall of Canada, Ltd., Toronto
Prentice-Hall of India Private Ltd., New Delhi
Prentice-Hall of Japan, Inc., Tokyo
Prentice-Hall of Southeast Asia Pte. Ltd., Singapore
Whitehall Books Limited, Wellington, New Zealand
10 9 8 7 6 5 4 3 2 1

Library of Congress Cataloging in Publication Data

Redfield, Malissa.
Scenes from country life.

1. Redfield, Malissa—Homes and haunts—Vermont.
2. Novelists, American—20th century—Biography.
3. Country life—Vermont. I. Title.
PS3568.E345Z475   813'.5'4 [B]   78-31856
ISBN 0-13-791632-9

For Robert, who brought us here.

For courtesy's sake, in telling this story, I have changed names and certain personal details. But these people and this place exist.

Malissa Redfield

CONTENTS

Finding the Country

The Fox

☙ Some tiny creature shrieking for its life woke us one night last week, and in an instant, so it seemed, we were out of bed and down the stairs. But as we opened the front door, the agonized voice fell silent. We hurried out into the silent darkness, too late. We were too late to intervene. If we had dared to.

The next morning we could find no sign of violent death, no bloody fur or feathers or splinter of fragile bone. A neat killer. Perhaps it was the fox. The fox is neat in taking the bones we leave by a certain stump near the woods at the edge of the upper field. If it is the fox. There's nothing the next day, not a sign.

We first saw the fox, early this summer, devouring the rank remains of a woodchuck, too ravenously intent on that rotten flesh to observe that we were coming toward it through the field. From a few feet away, we stood and watched it, a small, starved-looking, rusty-red, ragged-furred animal, until it suddenly sensed our presence and fled. We were sorry to have interrupted that wretched meal. But the next day there was nothing left of it, not a sign.

For the next few weeks we glimpsed the fox only at a distance. But then a month ago we had a spell of stunning heat, and perhaps that unaccustomed weather disturbed it. In those burning August twilights, its voice summoned us. From the safety of the screen door, we watched it pace back and forth in the grass just beyond our drive, glaring at us, so it seemed, and barking.

The fox's bark is high-pitched and harsh, loud and

raucous and strange. When I take our offerings to the stump, I don't linger. In the ceaseless rustling of the woods I imagine the presence of a small, famished animal with glaring eyes and a harsh voice and would rather keep my distance.

Life and death are the pervasive themes here, visible, undeniable. Pity the terror of its prey, but the fox kills to live. Man is the chief predator; pity the fox. We please ourselves by trying to appease its hunger, but it doesn't depend on and may not even go near what we choose to bring it. It is free of us, safe from us, beyond all our powers to intervene.

We had to wait almost four years to see a fox. They are rare here, we are told, because so many have died in epidemics of rabies. Or been shot. And those we see are likely to be rabid. There are other logical reasons and occasions for killing foxes. We have encouraged the shooting of woodchucks and allowed, or not tried to prevent, the hunting of deer. There is no logic in wanting the fox to survive. Except that they are rare, so we are told.

It could have been a fox stalking so near us the other night, but we don't know that it was and have no way of telling when, if ever, we will see one again. But perhaps we will look out early one morning soon and glimpse, as before, a small red animal trotting along in the distance. Or perhaps one evening we will hear that harsh voice again speaking for the unknown strength of whatever has defied or simply survived all our interventions.

We have built and planted here, and cut and cleared and enclosed, and are pleased with most of what we have done. But something strange to us has survived all our doings, something lovely in its strangeness, and we have hardly begun to guess at its strength. The four years since we first saw this country place are as crowded with impressions as a lifetime. We have crowded the elements of a new life into these years, and yet we are, above all, onlookers still, searching a world of life and death for signs.

11

Seeking the Country

❧ Sometimes, when our delight is greatest, like a child's on getting exactly what it wants, I think we must have been dreaming all our lives of having what we have found in the country. But the stuff of such dreams was hardly more than a trace in our suburban childhoods and grown lives in the city. *The country:* it was something in books, the subject matter of novelists and poets, a kind of fiction even when it was visible to the summer camper or the weekend visitor. The city was our natural element, our accepted reality and unquestioned necessity, and the source of most of the pleasures we had always depended on.

Then suddenly it seemed possible to leave the city, and without any serious discussion either of us can remember now, we decided to go. We never seriously considered any possibility except the one we chose: to find the country, an almost imaginary realm in our experience that we hardly knew where to seek.

All summer long, in ever-widening arcs northward from New York, we drove through New England. From camp days and weekends, we supposed that was where the country was, although we came to doubt it. We recognized a suburb when we saw one, or a commuter's village, and came to know the summer visitor's resorts and the immaculate retreats of gentlemen farmers and all the other country habitats of people much like ourselves. Perhaps, after all, we were mistaken, we sometimes thought, to want some of the country for ourselves when there seemed to be so little of it left. So little of what we seemed to want even though we couldn't have said just what that might be.

Sometimes one or the other of us was beguiled enough by a place to try to convert the other. Gil fancied for quite a while a large and elaborate house with formal gardens on a mountain peak in New Hampshire. We would be slaves to that place, I said, and we nearly quarreled. I had a weakness for cozy little cottages that Gil simply shook his head and smiled at. We hadn't been married to each other very long then and expressed disagreement more guardedly than we do now, but it was plain enough at times that each felt the other badly misunderstood the nature of what we were looking for.

Persisting, guided by little more than the poets' and novelists' images, we finally found it, a world we had never dreamed of inhabiting, a world filled with a child's profound delight in discovery.

Old Farm

❧ The *Times* ad is the first item in my first album. I never kept such memory books before, and now I have filled three. If we should have a fire, a particular fear in the country, I sometimes think I would forget every other possession and rush to save them.

The *Times* ad begins: *Whitcomb, S.E. Vt., sturdy century-old brick farmhouse with 170 beautiful acres*. We had answered dozens like it, traveling farther and farther from New York, and at the end of that summer four years ago we were seasoned to expect disappointment. We came up the hill for the first time, on a gray September afternoon, with little or no expectation of seeing something that we wanted. We have changed some of what we first saw almost beyond recognition, but we first wanted what we first saw, just as it was.

As Mrs. Howlett saw it. She painted a picture of the place a year or so before we answered that ad, while old Mr. Willard was still here. He must have been glad to see her come, an old friend and neighbor. It's a rather isolated spot, and he had been alone for years.

She must have stood her easel up in the front field at some distance from the house, because, without crowding, she got it all in. Not the view, of course, since her back was to it. But in her small canvas she got everything she intended to get: the red-painted brick house and frame wing and woodshed with the four elms in front, the barn and silo and sheds and pens, the small milk house and the doghouse, the chicken house out back by the white birch, the swing in the maple, and the road and fences and stone walls.

That painting hangs in the Howletts' kitchen, and when I'm there getting vegetables or eggs I study it, feeling again each time the powerful charm of what we first saw. None of the snapshots in my first album works so well. But my camera could catch only what was there. After I learned that she sometimes sold a picture, I asked Mrs. Howlett if she would consider selling us that one. She couldn't, she said. She was very fond of the old place and liked to be reminded of it.

Her fond memory faithfully rendered a neat, hardworking farmstead. My photographs show some of what we actually came upon that September afternoon. The silo sagging away from the barn and the barn's rusting roof. The sheds half down and the fences half gone and the barnyard a clutter of tools and machinery worn out years before. One of the elms was dead. Weeds were choking whatever had once been planted. But it was all still there then, the silo and the milk house, and even though we could see that its work was long finished, and though we knew nothing then of the place and its people, wherever we looked we felt a charmed sense of all the life that had been lived and the work that had been done here.

Some people who knew the old place may think, considering the changes we've made, that all we really cared for was the view. But if they do, they are mistaken.

We went into the house, which had been empty by then

for several weeks, since the summer's day when Clara Willard came and found her father lying in the yard, too ill to get up or say how long he had been there. Henry Willard was ninety-five then and had lived in the house for seventy-two years—a widower for the last ten, but always, before this illness, refusing to leave. Now I can begin to imagine the grief of his leave-taking. But what we saw then was simply a very old farmhouse, musty and worn and faded and emptied even of the furnishings of lives that had become a memory unknown to us. We wandered from room to bare room, silently, through the stillness of time stopped. All life here seemed to have fled.

And finally we went outside again and stood on the front steps. Facing the view. On our sitting room mantel now we have a copy of a photograph, which Clara Willard kindly gave us, taken of her father soon after he bought the place. He stands straight and young and smiling, on the front steps, gazing beyond the photographer at the sight that must have had something to do with his first wanting the place and with keeping him there to the last. It changes constantly as the weather changes, but what he saw then must essentially be the same still, the same long, wide, open, downward and upward sweep of fields, woods, hills, and sky. We saw it first on a gray day, with the fields dulled and the woods darkened and the distant hills half hidden by clouds, and never thought to regret the sun's absence or imagine that anything could be lovelier than what we were seeing. A view for all weathers. Yes, of course we cared for the view.

We walked out into the front field then and looked at the view, different in the field, and looked up at the sky, and turned and saw how the house, at the road's end, stands in the midst of open fields under the open sky. Gil said he wanted to have a look at the barn, and I went and sat in the swing in the maple and pushed myself to and fro, seeing how the view changed within the arc of the swing. For the first time, I began to think of how much needed to be done to the house, and that wasn't what we'd wanted, months of work and waiting, and there was far more land than we had any possible use for, and we hadn't counted on being so far from the city.

I saw Gil come out of the barn and slowed the swing to a stop as he came toward me. He looked up into the tree at the rigging of the swing and said, well, *that* seems to be in fine shape, and we looked at each other and laughed. Actually, he said in a moment, the barn isn't so bad, although it *needs work*. And the house, I said, seems sturdy enough, but it *needs work*, and we laughed again as if at the greatest joke and looked at each other with a delight that silenced us and deepened into dreaming joy.

Tom Sargent

As it turned out, we had a long while to think the whole matter over. There was an old road through the place of uncertain legal status that had to be resolved to clear the title. For almost three months, we were free to change our minds. Perhaps we might have considered the idea seriously if it hadn't been for Tom Sargent.

Not long before we left New York, a woman we met at a party, who had summered in Vermont, told us as if it were something she thought we ought to know that Vermonters hated the city people who came and bought their old places. *Hated* them. By then we had reason to believe otherwise, and I wished she knew Tom, for one.

Tom was there that first afternoon to show us around for the real estate agency, the first person we met in Whitcomb, which Sargents helped settle. Everyone else we met for a while we expected to be like Tom, he made such an impression on us.

A big, strong-looking, ruddy-faced man, Tom is past thirty now and still looks, in a certain way, like a boy. We see old men here who are still boyish in this way, the ones who look as though they have spent all their lives out of doors. They have clear skins and strong bodies, and in their eyes a kind of shy but intense brightness, the expression of a boy, a country boy, still marveling at the world. Tom, with any luck, will keep that brightness, and it's lovely. A girl I got to talking with in the supermarket line used that word. Oh, Tom Sargent, she said, he's lovely.

I remember that we didn't quite know what to make of Tom at first. He seemed so friendly. Not at all a city person's notion of a Vermonter. Cautiously, we took it for the professional friendliness of the real estate agent. But not for long. We don't have fixed notions about Vermonters now, if we ever did, but we have formed some impressions of the people around Whitcomb, and we learned, from Tom first, not to be wary of whatever they show of friendliness.

Tom is a cousin of the Willards, he told us that first afternoon, and had known the place all his life. He came out to ride the hay wagon when Mr. Willard still farmed, to pick apples, to skate on the pond up in the woods. And to hunt just as soon as he was old enough for a license. He said he guessed he'd walked every foot of the land at least once. Perhaps we'd like to walk around it with him, he said, before we made up our minds. But his smile made us realize that he already knew how we felt.

We spent hours with Tom, in the weeks that followed, walking the boundaries and seeing all the places on the land with memories for him. One hundred and seventy acres was an immense space to us then, a territory to which so experienced a guide seemed indispensable. Late summer turned

17

to fall, and then the leaves were gone, and then the first snow fell and melted, and still we walked, up hill and down, through the fields and the woods, along the course of brooks and around the pond, past old cellar holes and wells and over endless stone walls, talking and laughing sometimes, silent at others, never feeling tired, in weather that always seemed to be fair.

We drove up from the city almost every weekend and, except during deer season, Tom was always ready to come out with us. We met his wife, Kate, and over drinks and meals we learned a lot from the two of them about themselves and their lives and the life of the town. Our interest—our curiosity—was always evident enough, I suppose, but they always seemed pleased by it, as if by something pleasantly out of the ordinary. And that has been our experience with others since, around this small country town where most people already know, or think they know, so much about each other.

Gil occasionally expressed his exasperation as the weeks went by without a settlement of the title question, but Tom surely was never seriously worried that we might give up and go away. We could only think that he spent so much time with us because we were enjoying each other's company and doing something enjoyable and because, almost certainly because, he saw how much we cared for a place he cared about. He made us feel very welcome.

And so at last the day came, a cold, brilliantly sunny day in early December, when all the papers were signed, and we stood in front of the house in the snow, wearing for the first time the snowshoes Tom had helped us pick out and put on, and he took our picture. There we are in my first album, wearing our brand-new parkas and boots, poised to take our first steps on snowshoes, looking past Tom at the dazzling snow-covered fields, with such *smiles* on our faces.

A Story, A Memory

🌿 Seven children were born in the house to Henry and Anna Willard. Two died in childhood and a son was killed in the war. Two married daughters and a son live in distant towns, and we have met them only once, as they came back at different times to see what we had done.

I was the one who never got away, Clara Willard says, not complainingly but just as a matter of fact, as if it were natural to expect that one child in a family would stay close to home. As a young woman, after she went to work for the telephone company, she moved into an apartment in town. But she was always out at the farm, she says, especially when her mother and dad were getting on. But, of course, that was where she always *wanted* to be.

Tom arranged for us to meet Clara when we began to ask about the family. Mr. Willard was in a nursing home, not well enough to have visitors. But Clara, he told us after making some inquiry, would like to meet us; and so one Saturday afternoon in October, she came out to the place.

Every now and then I run into Clara in town. But I often mistake some stranger for Clara because the way she looks is so typical of certain older women here. The neatly curled gray hair and the silver-rimmed eyeglasses. The neat, solid, rather slow-moving bodies. The plain wash dresses and plain comfortable shoes. These women are attractive in their quiet indifference to style, their seeming imperviousness to change. Clara must be sixty, but I can't think that she has changed much in the last twenty years. Her skin is smooth and fresh and her smile young as a girl's.

We had misgivings on the day she was to come. Perhaps it was a tactless and pointless plan with nothing in store but mutual embarrassment. But as soon as we shook hands and Clara smiled, we were quite sure it was going to be all right. So you're the ones, she said, looking at us with such lively curiosity that we felt she might have been at least as interested in this meeting as we were. We were the ones, after all, the city people who had turned up in Whitcomb and were paying a price undreamed of a few years earlier for one of its worn-out farms.

Clara walked around the house with us that afternoon, remembering. That was where Mother's harmonium stood, in the parlor, and they used to sing. "Just a Song at Twilight," Dad's favorite, did we know it? And the dining room wallpaper—well, it was awfully faded now, but so *pretty* when it was new. And this was the girls' bedroom; it was a tight squeeze. And that one was the boys'. Mother used to keep the broody hens in this room when it was cold. The house was always full of sun; we must have noticed that. They knew how to set a house, the old people, so as to catch the sun.

Outside, we walked from building to building, and she talked about the decades when her mother was alive and her father was strong and well and the place was full of animals, her father liked to have a little bit of everything, and the fields were all planted and the farm was a decent living for them, not much money, but plenty to eat. Honey from their own hives. Their own fruit. Had we seen the red raspberry patch? And the apples, almost every tree a different kind, the old kinds, and the pears. Wait till spring, she said, looking off at the blaze of autumn color, and you'll see something pretty.

We walked out into the front field together and looked back at the farmstead, and for the first time it must have looked forlorn to her. She was silent for a moment and then she sighed and said, well, you know, if the war hadn't taken Eddie, he would have farmed, he was the farmer.

That was the closest she has come to expressing whatever she feels of irreparable loss. Except, perhaps, for something she said just after we had finished making all our

20

changes and she came out to have a look. She was warm in her praise, and finally she said she was glad we'd changed the place so much. Glad, she said, pausing, because now it didn't *remind* her.

But she has been generous with her remembering for our sakes. If she had doubts about our caring to hear whatever she cares to tell us, I think she settled them one day a year or so ago when she was looking through my albums. We had started getting the Whitcomb *Daily Sentinel* by mail in New York as soon as we decided on the place. When Mr. Willard died the following spring, I cut out the *Sentinel* obituary for my first album, and Clara came upon it there. She looked at me for a moment, appraisingly, seemed satisfied by what she found, and smiled her quick, bright, youthful smile.

Clara and Tom and Miss Mount and the Howletts and a few others have given us a sense of this place that matters to us and perhaps has some meaning beyond our grateful pleasure in what we know. They have been patient with our wish to know. Except for Miss Mount, people here, unless asked, don't talk much of the old days. Time goes too quickly, change comes too often, even here. Memory is the fragile thread of continuity. Our coming to this place marked the end of a certain long story that only a few people can tell. What we have been told, we remember; and will tell, if asked.

Old House, New House

❧ All our changes in the place weren't conceived at once. At first we imagined that the largest project we faced was to introduce what we can only think of, in our dependence on them, as essentials of life. But the Willards lived without them.

Sometimes when I feel oppressed by household tasks, I think of Mrs. Willard, and sometimes this shames me. Considering the ease of our own lives, we wonder, always, at the character that sustains relentlessly hard physical work, as it does still in the farm life here.

The only running water in the house, when we first saw it, was supplied in a rusty trickle by a single tap at a tiny kitchen sink, water that flowed through two hundred yards of lead pipe from a well in the upper field. There was a privy in the back of the woodshed. In Mr. Willard's last years, his children put in a furnace that would heat part of the downstairs. Two or three small stoves did the rest. Electricity was installed in the 1930's, and how Clara smiles when she tells of its coming, but the wiring was exposed, scanty, and ominously worn.

From Tom we learned that there was an architect in Whitcomb, and after seeing what he'd done with another old farmhouse, we got together with him. Paul Channing is native, too, and not much older than Tom, but perhaps his years away, at Harvard and with a Boston firm, made a different kind of man. He came back here for the chance to start his own practice, but we wonder how much longer he will stay. He gets on well with everyone, but it doesn't interest him, we feel, the manner of getting on well in this small world. His work interests him intensely, and for the rest he has the essentially detached, private attitude of the city person. We found our somewhat formal and always concentrated dealings with him well suited to what turned out to be a long, complex undertaking.

As it turned out, we had to be quite ruthless with our old house. Its roof and frame wing, its interior walls and floors, its stairway and doors and windows—all and more proved to be past preserving. I don't remember our being shocked as we made these discoveries. We were too involved, enthralled.

We have a sheaf of Paul's drawings bulky enough to fill

a big desk drawer. Gil says we built a new house. I prefer to think that we built a new house inside the old one, adding a new frame wing. We are middle-aged city people and hopelessly accustomed, I suppose, to the kind of comfort our country house was altered to provide. We saved what we could, including the century-old stone foundations, which can never be made completely waterproof. They glisten and drip in the cellar as they always have in the spring runoff, a reminder. And the sun streams in the new windows, and the windows look out on the view just as before, reminding us of what others must have felt for a century about the site of this house. Paul did a fine job, saving all he could of the old and planning the new with care for the future. Old and new, it's a lovely house. Good for another century, perhaps.

Bulldozer

❧ So, our building had to begin with destruction. What a day that was when the bulldozer came. A timely warm spell early in January had cleared away the snow, but the ground was still firm enough for that great machine. Ned Cutler was at the wheel, a man who plainly enjoys his work. Down came the old frame wing. Down came the silo and the sheds and the pens. Down came the chicken house out by the birch. And down came the milk house and the doghouse, despite our shouted, inaudible protests. Mr. Cutler was very sorry, but he hadn't gotten the word that we wanted them saved. Fortunately, he had gotten word not to touch the barn.

It happened so fast. By noon, Mr. Cutler was gone, along with the last truck carrying away the debris. We'd had a pile of the shed siding, bristling with rusty nails but possibly usable, put behind the barn. But the ground had been raked clean of almost every other sign of the long existence of what

23

now was gone, the decades of life ended in a morning. We stood on the bare ground between the barn and the brick house, in the sudden silence, feeling not sorry but rather solemn.

We had made our first mark, our first irreversible change. We didn't suppose even then that it mattered only to us what we did. Change is frequent here but still immediately visible and still visibly connected with particular human acts. In the town and the countryside we have seen a surprising number of changes, for better and worse, just in our short time here. But we always know, or can easily find out, whom to praise or blame. Nature is the only impersonal force freely acknowledged. The frost came too early; the rain came too late. But what we do we feel accountable for.

The Men on the Job

For weeks after the construction work began, I found myself spinning a daydream of the party we would have when it was finished, for all the men who had done the work and their wives and children. A picnic on a warm afternoon, with plenty of good food and cold beer. Perhaps a softball game, somehow a little music. The children playing, the women gathered in the shade to chat on a long, sunny summer afternoon.

I would like to think that this vision was innocent enough, however childlike, or anachronistic. We would be feasting the neighbors gathered for a barn raising. Certainly I was moved by some profoundly grateful feeling. But I suppose I was confused as a child might be by the fact that they seemed like such *nice* men, most of them, and so friendly; and surely they must share some of our pleasure at seeing the house take shape in their hands.

24

We came up from the city every week or ten days to see how the work was going. It was never going as fast as we had expected, but we would get over that inevitable disappointment and settle down to enjoy an hour of looking and talking. Because they were there the longest, we got to know the carpenters best, Mr. Tyson and Mr. Dubois. But we got to know a dozen men on the job well enough so that when we see them now we have something particular to say to each other, for a few moments at least. We still see many of them, from time to time, in the supermarket or the dentist's waiting room, at the high school band concert or the local steak place.

Most of them are in my first album, smiling for me. They always seemed amused, in a friendly way, by my wanting to photograph them. They must have sensed my confusion, tolerantly, with a smile for it. They felt they knew where we stood with each other, I suppose, no matter how much friendly talk we had about the work and the weather and the day's news and life in the country and life in the city and their families and ours. I go on puzzling about where we all stand here, the divisions against the common ground.

One unexpected, even astonishing, circumstance colored our feelings about that time and about all of our life here. We saw that, while the men took their own tools home with them, thousands of dollars worth of materials and equipment were left on the job with no attempt to safeguard them. At night or on the weekends for months, a thief with a truck could have made a sizable haul. So far as we know, not a two-by-four or a box of nails disappeared. Made uneasy, finally, by the delivery of all the household appliances, we demurred. It was perfectly all right, we were told, as it proved to be. Astonishing evidence to us of a world that still stands on some common ground.

I didn't tell Gil about my party notion until long after I had abandoned it, after the delays had begun to seem interminable and the cost of the work appalling, after some more or less intractable disagreements and misunderstandings, apparently ordained in this experience. The men doing the work weren't involved directly, but there was enough tension in the air for a while to make my pleasant daydream seem foolish. That was the way I told it to Gil eventually, as a foolish notion. It was too late then, in any case, but he thought about it and touched me by saying, what a nice idea, maybe we should have done it.

So there wasn't a party, but Mr. Tyson brought Mrs. Tyson around for a drink and a look at the house after we had moved in, and Dan Morse, the taper, came with his shy young wife, who seemed particularly pleased by our admiration for Dan's prowess on the metal stilts of his craft. Dave Fremont, one of the painters, stops by and has a beer when he is hunting in our woods each fall. And Mr. Dubois, the one who always seemed the most interested in what we were doing with the house, turns up once or twice a year. Sometimes he'll sit down and have a drink with us, but he always says he can't stay long. Just wanted to see if you're still liking the place, he says.

Three years after it was finished, we like it more than ever. Most of the work was done with greater than sufficient skill, some of it with exquisite care. And I look around the house even now and associate walls and floors, pipes and switches, brick, stone, and tile, with the faces and voices and smiles of particular human beings.

Mr. Rose

🙞 Mr. Rose belongs in this story although, he told me, he has never set foot in Vermont. He may by now have forgotten us, but our life is full of reminders of him.

Mr. Rose still, I assume, sells furniture at the one department store in New York that remains tolerably serene. I first met him soon after Gil and I were married, when I made some minor additions to our joint possessions. The grave attention he accorded my acquisition of a hall table and a bedroom chair I remembered at once when the time came to plan the move from five rooms into nine.

Most of our city furnishings seemed suitable enough for the country house, but we had two bedrooms, a study, and a sizable sitting room, where we also expected to have our meals when we were alone, to do from scratch. My one fixed idea on the subject was to try to have everything ready when the house was completed. I wanted to be ready to begin our new life. Confidently, I went back to Mr. Rose.

Mr. Rose is a small, graying, quiet man with a low, calm voice and an air of infinitely patient interest in his customer's wants. He is quiet but not silent. He has informed himself about what he has to sell and imparts his knowledge in an unhurried way that I found helpful, particularly because it gave me ample time to reflect. We would stand contemplating a table or bed or chair together, Mr. Rose talking of its merits or possible limitations, and I, half listening, soothed by the sound of his voice, sinking into a vision of a room, a meal, a guest, a whole new life.

We spent hours that way, steadily working through my list. I got Gil to come around and be in on the major choices, but while he genuinely liked Mr. Rose, he felt no desire, or need, to linger. These final deliberations were far brisker, but Mr. Rose proved perfectly adaptable to them and even, I thought, looked with favor on this quick decisiveness of a busy man called away from his office. I was always just as glad when Gil left.

I couldn't take as an impersonal exchange this consultation on the necessities of daily domestic life. Gradually, Mr. Rose and I had begun to wander from the business directly at hand to personal matters. I don't know what he remembers now, if anything, about the private concerns of Mrs. Gilbert Lovell, but I still find myself wondering occasionally whether his daughter, who was at Barnard, went on to medical school as planned, or whether his son, who had dropped out of New York University to play his guitar with a rock group, ever went back to school. Mr. Rose still has, I assume, his summer place in the Catskills. I remember very well his gentle attempt to warn me against what I might face in the country. He said he feared he took it for granted for years that his wife should entertain visitors all summer. I was touched, and incapable then of believing that visitors could be anything less than a delight. I was furnishing two extra bedrooms expressly for guests.

This collaboration was just as fruitful as I had imagined it would be. Gil and I found a few things elsewhere: a nice old chest on Third Avenue, the fireplace brass on Allen Street, some rugs at an auction. My generous father gave us the desk that had been my mother's and the Victorian love seat and chair that were made for his own parents. But it was Mr. Rose who enabled me to carry out my plan.

Occasionally now when I see a house filled with nothing but handsome old pieces, thoughtfully accumulated, I suppose, one at a time over years, I feel a little sorry for my impatience. But not really. I wanted those brand new things, as fresh and new as the life we were beginning. And I wanted to be free to start living the visions that had taken on some of their form so naturally while I communed with Mr. Rose.

I went back to see him a few months after we had moved when I was in the store again shopping for clothes. As soon as I stepped off the elevator on the furniture floor, I caught sight of him. He was standing with a smiling middle-aged woman who reminded me of myself, their heads bowed over a book of fabric samples, a look of rapt attention on both their faces. When I had come close enough, I heard Mr. Rose's familiar voice. I paused, feeling like an intruder. Finally, he glanced up and recognized me. Excusing himself to his customer, he came over and we smilingly shook hands. We exchanged friendly queries, I told him how much we were liking everything, and then I said I must go. I was conscious of the woman waiting, and of Mr. Rose waiting, too. I had interrupted something personal.

Country Neighborhood: Up and Down the Road

෴ While the work on the house went ahead, we were getting to know our country neighborhood, although not yet any of the people in it. The people, in those winter months, were rarely visible to us. I suppose we were more visible to them than we realized. The *Sentinel* had reported our purchase of the place and then the start of the work in items appearing in a weekly column under the byline Ada Mount. It's hard for me to remember now that there was a time when her name meant nothing to us.

We were in such an excited state at first that we scarcely noticed certain features of our neighborhood. We still take wry pleasure in sometimes describing for visitors the route to our house in terms of these landmarks. At the turn off the highway onto the road running through our neighborhood, you'll see what looks like a big greenhouse but is actually a sewage treatment plant. Then comes the trailer park. Then the barn that fell down ten years ago. Then a farmyard full of junked cars. Then a house that apparently is being repainted, except that the white part and the green part are almost equally weathered. Then a tiny red house that seems to be made of tar paper, and that is where you take the left fork up Henry Willard Road to our house.

This description is accurate enough, so far as it goes,

although the junked cars have recently disappeared in the wake of a new town ordinance. There are twice as many trailers in the trailer park as there were when we first saw it. The hulk of the barn decays imperceptibly. Mr. Burton is not about to finish painting his house and have his property tax raised.

And yet the effect of most of this stretch of the road is lovely. It is a well-made gravel road of a pleasing sandy brown. It runs through deep woods and open fields and by pastures where cows and horses graze. I know a bank where wild roses bloom, then tiger lilies, then Michaelmas daisies, according to season. Ferns and forget-me-nots fill the shady ditches all summer long.

The LeBeau, Howlett, and Putnam houses are snug and spruce. The tiny red house, which is not actually made of tar paper but of some sort of asphalt siding, has taken on, in our feelings for it, the charm of its owner, Miss Mount. And she has the prettiest hollyhocks.

The proximity of the trailer park was disconcerting to us at first, faintly menacing even. A kind of habitation, so far as we knew, to which only the desperate would have recourse. Now we are not so ignorant. This particular trailer park, called the Mobile Homestead, is a decent place to live, from all we hear, and within the stark limitations, it is becoming a pleasant place to look at. Walks are put in, trees and shrubbery planted. The children have a playground. A big common garden flourishes each summer. Familiar to us now, the trailer park simply is what it is, an essential element of life here, answer to a need, and not by any means the most desperate answer.

A mile or so beyond the fork where you turn up to our place, the road acquires a character more consistent with the expectations of prosperous city people. Some of the handsomest old houses around Whitcomb are to be found, spaced at agreeable intervals, along the next several miles. The most casual observer will conclude that there is more money here for amenity, although nothing like great wealth is in evidence. This is our neighborhood, too, and many of its inhabitants, the Talcotts, the Grays, the Forsters, and others, have been as friendly to us, although in certain different ways, as a number of our neighbors on the lower part of the road.

Nature was generous with all of our neighborhood. But the observer judging only by what is man-made will certainly find the more prosperous part of the road more consistently pleasing. When we first became aware of it, this visual contrast was striking to us, and we drove by the handsome old houses a little wistfully. How comfortable to see on all sides nothing but such signs of prosperity. Our house, centered in its own hilly land, is out of sight of any other dwelling, except miles away across the river valley, and so we could feel unconcerned enough about the neighborhood. But still it made us thoughtful, this contrast in it, and its unknown meaning in our new life.

If we thought about it at all beforehand, I suppose we assumed that our neighbors in the country would be people more or less as prosperous as ourselves. And if we had a house in the midst of the handsome houses, that is the way it would be. We might not even have considered the lower part of the road our neighborhood. We could have been cut off from a great part of what gives our life here meaning.

The loveliness around all of us is common ground. The prosperous and the modestly comfortable and the struggling and the feckless share it in a way that matters, perhaps profoundly. We and our neighbors, up and down the road, live as we can and will and know how to, and the man-made consequences vary accordingly. But the loveliness is triumphant still, the great impartial grace for every life.

31

Spring

❧ That first spring is fixed in my memory as the season's essence. Spring has surely been as stirring a time each year since then, but we perceive it differently. It is such a demanding season now in the garden that I am far less attentive to its paramount events and sometimes even miss entirely its more delicate and transitory signs. In that first spring, with the ground around the house devastated by the construction work, the garden was nothing but the plans coming from the drawing board of our landscape architect. But the house was emerging from its unfinished state. We could begin to see clearly what it promised to become, and this stage in its evolution seemed to correspond very well to what we observed of the season when so much is unfinished and absorbed in the process of *becoming*.

That spring began early, although we didn't realize it. By now we have learned to expect a covering snow in April. That year, the last snow fell early in March. The frost left the ground in mid-March, the ground turned to mud, and water rushed down every slope and stood in every hollow, and then by early April, as if a strong hand had wrung it out, the ground was firm again and the rushing water confined to its normal course in brooks and streams. Whenever it happens, this is the indispensable first stage, this great, wet emptying out of winter from the earth.

We began to come up still more often as the work and the season advanced, to miss as little as possible of what was occurring in each. But since we weren't continuously present, the changes ordered by spring seemed more abrupt than we now know them to be and more striking. I remember how the air changed, so suddenly it seemed, from hard, dry cold to soft, wet warmth, the most expressive of all the changes, in a way, of this time of most complete transformation. When the very air changes, something radical is happening to the world.

But I remember how we noticed, long before any green began to show, that in certain lights the woods suddenly seemed to be darkly, redly aglow. We half thought we were imagining it, but now we await each year this unmistakable sign, the deep flush of swelling buds. Something profound is happening then. And I remember our first glimpse of returning creaturely life, a huge, excited flock of blackbirds that paused for a day in the tops of the elms. And I remember hearing for the first time that most compelling sound of life reborn, the nightly shrilling of the peepers up at the pond. And of course I remember finding the first violets: expecting to find them and yet being taken by surprise.

Spring lasts so much longer than we had realized in the city, a good three months of advance, pause, retreat, and advance again toward the climax, the weeks in late May and early June when the lilacs, the apple trees, and then the roses come into bloom. That first spring happened to be one of the grand ones for flowering, unsurpassed since. We discovered in the lower field, where it seems a barn once stood, a lilac twenty feet across, a fragrant purple mound, when the time came, alive with bees. And out by the white birch, a white lilac, luminous after a rain. And just within sight of the house, more than thirty apple trees, old, gnarled, unpruned trees all at once hidden that spring, to the least twig, by shimmering clouds of bloom. And the wild roses, visible in the most unexpected places when the delicate flowers showed on the tough, thorny stems.

I took some photographs, faint images of that prodigal beauty, but a reminder. Now I tend to observe the progress of spring most closely in relation to what is happening among the plants we have put in. That has its acute pleasures, too, watching one's own garden come back to life, but it's hard to avoid feeling anxiously proprietary, responsible. I hover over the tender green, full of doubts about the adequacy of my

33

care, uneasily conscious of the hazards that are beyond my control. In that first spring, all seemed freely given, all was revelation, free of warning or command. The voices of the crows in March, a field full of robins in April, still remind me of this time.

Now we know just where to find the hepaticas and the lady's slippers, and we expect to see the pastures turn blue-white when the bluets bloom. Then it was all an astonishment, an experience of wonder impossible to repeat but always to be remembered as a time when our response was truest to the character of the season. Spring overtook the world, and we were carried along with a sense of pure delight in nature's power.

The Death of Arthur Parsons

൨ We have one dark memory of that radiant time. The death of Arthur Parsons. We scarcely knew him, but we had made an agreement with him that seemed to promise a long and friendly acquaintance.

Clara had told us about him during our first meeting with her. After her father sold his herd, Arthur Parsons was the one who took their hay. He had a dairy farm not far away. We weren't to feel under any obligation; she just thought we might be interested.

We had hardly begun to consider the use of any of the land. There were thirty acres or more of hayfield, and we understood that at least they ought to be kept mowed. Clara seemed to think well of Arthur Parsons.

Gil called him, and one afternoon that first fall he came around, a tall, thin, gentle-looking man in early middle age, with a formal manner that seemed to be a mark of considerable shyness. We liked him at once, and he gradually began to seem more at ease with us as the three of us stood talking in the front field. We asked him about his farm and the state of farming around Whitcomb, and he asked us a shy question or two about where we were from and what had brought us here. After ten or fifteen minutes, I wasn't surprised to hear Gil say that we would be very glad if he cared to continue the haying. He said with a quick smile that he'd been hoping to, and he and Gil shook hands on it. We hadn't asked Clara about the terms of his arrangement with her father, but exchanging the hay for the mowing seemed fair enough to us, at least until we'd had time to learn more about the possibilities of our land. We were glad to think of something continuing as before.

One afternoon not long afterward, Arthur Parsons came by with his father. Taking Dad for a little drive, he said, as he helped his father from the car. We noticed the care he took with the frail, stooped old man. He'd been thinking, he said, if it was all right with us, that he'd bring some manure up soon so as to have it ready to spread when spring came. And we happened to be there when he brought a load, leaving a big, dark, rich-looking pile by the edge of the upper field. We stood and chatted for several minutes in the bright sun of an Indian summer day. He said he'd been thinking, if it was all right with us, of putting corn in the upper field. He said he didn't have much good corn land of his own. Gil said that sounded fine.

That was the last time we saw him. One night in late February he went out to his milk house with a hunting rifle and shot himself. We saw the story in the *Sentinel* three days later in New York. He was forty-two and never married, the story said. His mother was dead, and he and his father had lived alone together on the farm.

That weekend we were back in Whitcomb. Perhaps if we hadn't met the old man, it wouldn't have occurred to us to pay a call. But it seemed like the right thing to do. Gil telephoned, and a sister of Arthur Parsons who seemed to know who we were said, yes, to come.

There were a number of people at the house when we arrived, mostly sisters and brothers, it seemed. And the old man, silently weeping. We said something about being *sorry*, and something about *such a fine man*, trying to say *something* to that silent, helpless grief.

One of the brothers came outside with us when we left. Dick Parsons, a different kind of man from Arthur, much easier, or so he seemed when we got to know him later. He asked us then if we'd care to look around the barns, and of course we said we would. We guessed he wanted someone to talk to or just to think out loud to.

Afterwards we heard several explanations for Arthur Parsons' suicide. There was something about a boy who'd been like a son to him, helping him after school and summers, who'd gone off and joined the Navy. And there was something even more speculative about a woman. But Dick Parsons probably understood as well as anyone could.

Art was the one, he said that day, who never got away. We remembered that phrase. For Arthur Parsons, it seemed to have meant a life he had never really chosen. The others had gone, and he was left, the youngest, like it or not, to carry on the farm. Oh, he worked at it, Dick Parsons said, worked like a driven man. When the dairy inspectors came they couldn't even find a dusty light bulb to mark him down for. He hardly left the farm, hardly saw anybody but his Dad, never found a girl. But no one ever asked whether it was what he *wanted*.

They had to sell the herd right away, since there was no one to do the milking, but they didn't sell the farm equipment until the spring. We went to the auction, on a fine May morning, vaguely thinking there might be something we could use. There was a big crowd and a refreshment van, and the farmers from miles around bid everything in while we stood bemused by the lively, almost festive scene. Old Mr. Parsons was there, greeting everyone in a friendly way, looking like himself again. And when we saw Dick Parsons, he surprised us by saying, I'm going to get to those fields of yours this summer.

And he did. They had saved a tractor and mower out of the sale, so as to be able to keep their own fields down. In July he came and mowed our fields, leaving the hay, since they had no use for it. We were too surprised to know what to do. We had expected to have to pay someone to mow, and Gil finally said so to Dick. He dismissed the subject with brisk finality. You were counting on Art, he said, and it makes me feel better to do it.

Next spring the Austins took over the fields. They had no interest in the manure that Arthur Parsons brought because of the inevitable weed seeds in it. More modern farmers, they like chemical fertilizers. I've been using the manure in my garden and, four years after the Parsons cows consumed them, the weed seeds still germinate. There is a pretty little geranium that is particularly irrepressible. But it's grand stuff, that manure, and I don't like to see how the pile is dwindling.

The police statistics in the town report include two or three suicides every year. I see these figures and wonder again about Arthur Parsons. Such a death seems stranger here, where nature so visibly commands life to be lived out, than it does in the city.

Mr. Parsons lives alone on the farm now. No one can persuade him to leave.

Harry Goodwin

❧ The landscape plan called for two cemented retaining walls and a free-standing dry wall. Our mason quoted a price on these walls that suggested he didn't especially care if he got the job. Tom Sargent told us he knew of a boy who'd had a little experience with walls and was looking for work. And so it was that Harry Goodwin came to test his sense of vocation.

Harry had finished school that June. He was eighteen but still very much a boy in looks, fair and blue-eyed and downy-cheeked, a country boy with a sweet, trustful smile. Practically the first thing he told us was that his wall experience hadn't amounted to much. But he'd liked the work, he said, and would like to give our job a try.

The stone for the walls was to be gathered from the immense supply available in the old walls that run all over our place. We had acquired by then a four-wheel-drive Blazer, a rough cross between a truck and a station wagon that seemed suitable for a variety of country uses as yet unknown and proved its worth in its first task of hauling the stones. Gil's son Steve came up when college ended for the summer, and he and his father spent hours together, one sunny week in June, filling up the back of the Blazer at the old walls and bringing their carefully chosen load back to the sites of the new. It was heavy work, but I could see they were enjoying every minute of it and envied them. It was the first job on the place in which our own labor was involved.

The landscape plan included sketches of the new walls and gave their approximate dimensions, but that was all Harry had to go on. He knew how to handle cement, and we had rented a power-driven cement mixer. Gil and Steve had supplied him with a pile of good flat slates for the dry wall and another, larger pile of more or less oblong small boulders, mostly granite, for the retaining walls. He was ready to set to work on a morning when Gil and I had to start back to New York. Gil helped him sort out some of the biggest slates for the first course of the dry wall, and then we drove off, leaving him studying the stone with a look of somber concentration.

Gil speculated on the meaning of that look several times while we were in the city. It was nice to think that Harry took the job seriously. But perhaps, after all, it was going to be too much for him. He was such a likeable boy. It would be hard to tell him if we weren't satisfied.

We timed our return a week later for an hour at the end of the day when we were sure Harry would be gone. As soon as we saw the beginning of the dry wall, Gil's uneasiness vanished. It wasn't as far along as he had thought it might be, but what was there was a fine piece of work.

When we complimented Harry the next day, he turned a bright rose, the truest blush I've ever seen. Obviously, he was pleased, but he was just as plainly embarrassed. He thanked us and began to apologize almost in the same breath. He knew it wasn't going fast enough, he said. Of course, it wasn't placing the stones that took the time. It was picking them. He'd stand and study one and then another, and he'd start to take up the first one and then the second one, and then the first one would look better after all, or maybe neither was just right, and that's the way it went. Or didn't go.

He seemed so dejected finally that we half expected him to say he wanted to give the job up. But Gil hastened to assure him that greater speed wasn't essential, we renewed our compliments, and gradually he began to look as if his good spirits had been restored.

Occasionally again, in the next weeks, he expressed concern about his progress, but as the dry wall was completed and the retaining walls were begun, we felt he was acquiring proper pride in an admirable accomplishment. He began to grow a beard, an unexpected transformation, as it filled out,

39

of a boy to young man and a sign, we thought, of a growing sense of mastery. He invited his mother and father around to see the walls, and then he invited a girl, occasions when we were present to see him smilingly accept abundant praise.

We felt happy on our own account, getting a good job done at a fair price. And we had the pleasure of thinking that we had provided the means by which a promising boy had discovered what he could do, well and enjoyably, to earn his living. Since we knew by then a number of people in the local building trades, we hoped that we could help Harry get started as a mason. One day, as the work neared its end, Gil raised the idea with him. And Harry would have none of it.

He blushed again, the rose glowing above the thick blond beard, in that earlier combination of pleasure and embarrassment. He thanked us again and again for our interest, and he was awfully sorry, he said, but he just couldn't consider it. No, he said, he wasn't cut out for it. It worried him too much, having to decide, having to *choose*, every minute of the time. He'd enjoyed working for us and was glad we were pleased, but he was sure he would be happier in a job where he didn't have to figure it all out for himself every minute. Reluctantly, we were persuaded that nothing we could say would change his mind.

That fall, Harry went to work as an apprentice machinist with one of the plants in Whitcomb that make industrial machinery. I'm sure he is good at what he does, and he says he likes it. He says he likes being with the other men. He was laid off once when orders were slow, but still, as he says, it's probably more dependable than the building business. For safety reasons, he was required to shave off his beard, but it didn't turn him back into a boy.

Every few months he comes to see us. Or to see the walls. Now he says he can scarcely believe it's his own work.

We have a joke about that with him. But perhaps we will surprise him one day.

There is one stone in one of the retaining walls that is considerably larger than the rest. It is too big, in fact, the one really noticeable flaw. But its wide, flat surface would be a fine place for an inscription. *Young Harry Goodwin made these excellent walls.*

Settling

Arrival

∾ The rugs, back from the cleaners, were piled in the hall all summer. Cartons full of books and dishes stood in every corner of the apartment. We lived through a series of postponed moving days, until finally we could wait no longer for the house to be ready. Our lease was expiring, and in September we had to go.

It rained as we left New York and rained the next day in Vermont. The painters were half finished. The house was filled with the dust and debris of building. Around it there was nothing as yet but sodden and littered earth.

It was a disconcerting transition. We were beginning a promising new life. A year had made its setting more familiar, but in ways that seemed to emphasize how different it was to be. With a year to prepare, we had expected to be *ready*.

A month of furious activity accomplished more than we had dared imagine it could. Room by room, the house was brought to completion to the last switch plate, closet pole, and doorknob, the last stroke of paint. Room by newly painted room, we washed and cleaned and unpacked and arranged, settled the largest and even most of the smallest of details, lamps, pictures, books, objects, all given a place. Room by room, the house emerged, bright, fresh, orderly, inviting, pleasing us more than we had dared to hope it would, ready at last.

I remember thinking of how our effort resembled the readying of a stage for a play. A play called *Life in the Country*, with a beginning to be signaled as precisely and formally as by the raising of a curtain. Even with a year of preparation, our sense of unreality was strong. Real life was our old city life. Our old selves, it seemed, our city selves, were of uncertain relevance to the roles we were about to assume. But when the scene had been properly set, the play was to begin.

I remember from that month, before the curtains were hung, how the brightness of the rising sun filled our bedroom. Every corner of the room was suddenly flooded with light on those clear fall mornings, and we would wake at once, even from the weariest sleep, with a sense almost of disbelief in the extravagance of the effect, the unfamiliar, overwhelming radiance of the sun at daybreak. We couldn't sleep in that light, but after we hung the curtains, I missed it. Its intensity seemed fitting, like the brilliance of a kind of stage light.

And I remember our looking out the windows as we worked and longing for the fields and woods. It turned out to be a month of exceptionally fine fall weather, and we longed to be out of doors. We persevered, consoled by the emerging charm and comfort of the house and our growing sense of being at home in it. We worked and looked out the windows and slowly began to understand that these days were part of our lives, a continuation of reality, largely unknown to us still but daily more familiar and gradually to be comprehended not by actors but by our old selves, ready or not.

Landscape

∾ The transformation that was occurring out of doors while we got the house in order persisted in seeming like stage-setting, perhaps because we had so little part in it. We couldn't name most of the greenery that was being moved into place, nor imagine the intended effect of it. We hoped we would be pleased.

Learning as we went along, we were involved with Paul Channing in almost every aspect of the planning of the house. But we had accepted almost without question Andrew Page's landscape design. We were too ignorant to ask questions, and there didn't seem to be time, in the midst of our preoccupation with the house, to learn.

Mr. Page's manner doesn't encourage casual displays of ignorance. Of all the people we have worked with here, he comes closest to being the laconic Vermonter. We were daunted as well as reassured by the impression of solid authority he creates with a few words. We were flattered, even, by his tacit refusal to attempt our education, and pride seemed to require us to pretend we needed none. We were clear about the formal elements of the design, the location of walks and walls, of trees and shrubbery and lawn. The rest we took on faith, not even understanding what a large act of faith it was.

With the landscaping under way, I made my first awkward effort to acquire the knowledge which even then I felt would be part of a profound new pleasure. Pride or diffidence kept me from asking the men from the nursery what that tree or bush was they were putting in. After they left for the day, I went around with the drawings on which all the plantings were named. Arrowwood—so that's what it looked like. Coralberry and snowberry. Potentilla, witch hazel, and autumn olive, hawthorn and Manchu cherry. There they were, the living expression of those lovely names. Or so the drawings said. It was a start, trying to remember the names.

Last of all the lawn was delivered. A very long flatbed truck came up the hill one morning, laden with exquisitely neat rolls of turf which, duly laid down, formed deep, smooth, emerald green carpeting, front and back. It seemed like such a reversible process. I imagined the truck returning and the lawn going back down the hill. We walked on it with gingerly steps, anxious not to mar its perfection.

I have to look at my photographs to remember how everything looked then, and why we felt both more than pleased and vaguely uneasy. Uncanny perfection is what I see in all those pictures. Not a weed or a broken twig, not a sign of unruly growth. Deep in mulch, each carefully pruned tree or shrub stands at a proper distance from its neighbors. We could hardly reproach Mr. Page for such a meticulous achievement. It never entered my head to ask him how it was supposed to look in a year or three years. I think I anxiously assumed that, given proper care, it should look exactly the same.

Three years later, the lawn is the only element of the landscaping that has responded to our care by remaining in something close to its pristine state. It is nearly perfect enough still to go right back to the turf company. Freshly mowed, it creates an illusion of control that soothes me when I consider the rest. The rest is marvelous to me but not soothing.

No shrub or tree has grown to less than half again its newly planted size. Some are two or three times as large. All encroach upon each other, most with seemingly relentless vigor. Weeded and weeded again, countless times, the mulched beds lost their inviolate look, which I had taken to be eternal, in the first summer. At some point in the second summer, I at last began to understand the fact that not even through one season, scarcely for a single week, could I expect to preserve a changeless effect. So elemental a discovery was like a revelation, not soothing but exhilarating. I didn't relax my care but at last began to understand its aim, the aim of the living plant, to sustain growth in the midst of change.

So, the bittersweet surges up the chimney, the spreading yew spreads across the walks, spiraea blocks the light from the living room, cotoneaster rasps against the screens outside the sitting room, the white pines cast longer and longer shadows. Just as the house already shows signs of wear and weathering, so the plants begin to run wild. Something will have to be done eventually, I suppose, about both situations. But now we are glad to see that house and grounds no longer form a kind of island of carefulness and constraint. Like the fields and woods with which they have merged, they are slowly, ceaselessly changing. The house weathers, the deeply rooted plants run a little wild.

I have long since learned all the names, and far more. What filled my thoughts, I wonder now, before I learned so much about gardening? Gardening! That first fall I had barely begun to guess at the power of its claims.

The Barn

∾ In their newness and neatness, house and grounds looked nearly suburban at first. But just beyond them stood the old barn, which we'd let alone, almost.

Paul proposed quite seriously that we take the barn down. We would get far more of the view, as he said. It was scarcely fit for animals any longer, and for what it would cost to fix it up properly, we could build a smaller modern one. If we wanted to someday, if we ever wanted animals. Someone might even pay to take the old one down, for the hand-hewn, pegged beams and weathered siding.

That was the only important idea of Paul's that we rejected. To his surprise, we wouldn't even consider it. Gil seemed a little surprised that I wouldn't consider it. But I think we have always felt almost the same way about the barn.

We had its rusting metal roof painted a reddish brown, which scarcely changed its appearance, and for safety reasons we had the old wiring and water pipes replaced. Gil had the nice idea of putting three small, square windows that were taken from the house in the side of the barn that faces the house, and they look as if they had always been there. That is all we have done to the barn, little enough in relation to its needs.

The barn is one of the first things I see every morning when I open our bedroom curtains. The side facing the house is especially reassuring as seen from our room. The wood has aged to dull silver and bronze, but it seems to be intact. The ridge line of the roof looks perfectly straight. After a stormy night, I study the roof line with care, knowing what I know about the state of the barn.

A few boards are missing from the gables, and the lean-to shed at the back has lost a door. But except for the splintering sills, the outside of the barn from every vantage point makes an impression of soundness that leaves me unprepared, still, for the effect inside.

Mr. Tyson and Mr. Dubois checked the barn over for us and assured us that, so long as we take care of the roof, it will go on standing indefinitely just as it is. I remind myself of this expert judgment when I go inside and see the tumble of stones where the foundation fell in along the north end, the braces under the cross beams pulling away from the posts, the dust rising under my feet from the crumbling wooden floors, the daylight filtering through on all sides, through all the places, not so noticeable from the outside, where the battens are gone from the boards.

I look up at the ridge line, marked by the metal track which carried the hayfork, and it seems to be perfectly straight. Somehow. I know too little about the way this barn was built, more than a century ago, and so must take its survival on faith. I look up at the rafters, meeting high above my head. The large, open, ascending space defined by them is familiar, the kind of space designed in sacred buildings to encourage faith. When I look up at the rafters, so roughly cut and yet straight, so heavy and yet raised so high, I believe the barn will stand.

The barn isn't entirely empty of its past. It still houses a large, ancient, and helpless-looking silage cutter, a crank-type butter churn lacking its crank, a variety of burst barrels, bottomless buckets, feed boxes half unhinged. Useless remnants no one ever bothered to get rid of, if only because there's so much room in the barn. Nor will we, if only for the same reason. Or because we have so few relics. The maker's name for the churn is still faintly visible: *Surprise No. 2.* We will never need the churn's space for our casual and inconsequential uses of the barn. Storage for the lawn furniture and gardening equipment, for our shiny little power lawn mower. How the barn has come down in the world, or in human service, sheltering no creatures but birds, mice, woodchucks.

The barn itself is a relic, but one of uncommon beauty. I have become a close observer of old barns, staring at them from the car as we drive around the countryside. A slightly morbid part of my interest is to try to appraise their degree of decreptitude and make comparisons. I notice whether the straighter, stronger-looking barns have well-kept roofs, and I take a certain comfort when I see how much neglect of other kinds a barn will stand up under.

It took me a while to realize that not all old barns are beautiful, my city person's calendar-art notion. Making comparisons, I began to see how the simplest form can be clumsy and the aging even of fine form only a descent into slovenliness. Our barn has aged with grace, but its size and shape are graceful, too, its lines satisfying to the eye from every angle. It must have been beautiful from the start, perhaps by chance, perhaps because someone knew and cared. Probably its beauty has always given pleasure.

Paul took us for the city people we are, with a fondness

for views and no apparent use for a barn. Granting the distinguished appearance of our barn, he still assumed we would feel it got in the way, as old barns often seem to. We couldn't explain why, when we were being so ruthless with the house, we were determined to spare the barn. But now the reasons seem clearer.

The barn is more than a link with the past. To preserve it is to pay homage not just to times gone by but to the life that some of our neighbors stubbornly continue here. Barns as old as ours are kept in use. Gil, I know, is still tempted by the idea of animals. But whatever we decide to do with our barn, at least we can make certain it outlasts us. We keep an eye on the roof, and as soon as we can, we'll do something about the foundation and the braces.

My heart sinks when I think we might have agreed with Paul. The house is handsome, but we know where we are when we look at the barn.

Miss Mount

❧ Miss Mount belongs here in this account, if only because she was the first person on the road to come to call, while we were still unpacking. Others came to the house at this time, but not to call.

Ted Putnam stopped by one evening. No, he wouldn't come in; he just wanted to say that if there was anything he could do to help us get settled, we must be sure to let him know. This offer seemed so sincerely and kindly meant that we thought for several days about how we might respond to it. But we couldn't bring ourselves to impose on a stranger— our city view of the matter.

Mrs. Howlett telephoned one morning, introduced herself in her shy way, and said she wouldn't have bothered us but she was collecting in our neighborhood for the heart fund. She came up the hill to get our contribution—neither too large nor too small, I hoped—but she wouldn't come in, not when we were so busy, she said, with a quick, interested glance at the house that made me feel she would gladly come in another time.

We startled John and Louise Talcott on the lawn one afternoon as they stood studying the front of the house. They hadn't realized we'd moved in, they said, with the rather formal apologies we would have made in such circumstances to strangers. They told us they were neighbors, gesturing in the direction of the more prosperous part of the road. We were almost certain they were former city people. Of course they wouldn't come in, but they were perfectly friendly in a guarded way that we thought we understood.

Miss Mount knocked at our door one day, just as we were finishing lunch, and came in without a moment's hesitation. She was already a familiar figure. We had seen her often that summer, as we drove past the little red house, working in her garden in a neat, faded print house dress and fraying straw hat. She had begun an exchange of waves and smiles that gave us a feeling of welcome each time. It seemed natural to find her at our door, and then sitting in our still disordered sitting room with a glass of ginger ale, but we also had a sense of event, one commanding our full attention, in this first real encounter with a near neighbor.

I remember wondering that day how old Miss Mount was. From seeing her at work in her garden, spading and hoeing and carrying a full pail of water in each hand, I had thought she could be seventy, a white-haired but youthful seventy. Sitting close to her for the first time and seeing the lines in her face and hands, the innumerable fine lines in the worn and weathered skin, I suddenly thought that she might be older than anyone I had ever known before. We still don't know exactly how old she is, but everyone thinks she is well past eighty. And yet she had walked up the hill that day to call on us.

We had already learned that she was our local reporter, and that was the ostensible reason, the polite warrant, for her call, to obtain some account of our move to Whitcomb for her column. But her curiosity about us was entirely personal, not about our histories, the facts of our lives, but in a more fundamental sense about who we were, what kind of people we were. She was studying us, we could see, in a friendly but searching way. It was unexpected but enjoyable, this keen scrutiny, almost flattering, to think that we should matter, that we newcomers, strangers, should be so interesting in some way to this clear-eyed, strong old woman who, she told us, had been born and lived all her life in the red house.

From Miss Mount that first afternoon we began to understand something of the ways in which we neighbors figure in each others' lives. She is unabashed in revealing the interest everyone has, not in prying into privacy or pressing for intimacy, but in knowing what to expect, for good and ill, from each man, woman, or child who, in the country sense, is a neighbor. Now this interest seems natural to us among so few people, no more than two dozen on a mile or so of road, most of whom were born here or long ago came to stay.

Miss Mount disposed of the formal business at hand with some brief questions. We felt with her, as with others, that she has no use, no place in her thoughts, for the remote and novel facts of lives spent in a city. She took her soundings that afternoon, not by seeking to draw us out, but just by seeing what it was like to sit and talk with us. At first a little diffidently, we found ourselves asking the questions. Soon we realized that she thought it only proper that we, the newcomers with everything to learn, should want to know what she has to tell; and with a growing sense of astonished pleasure, we listened.

Miss Mount's history can be stated in a few lines. Her father, a carpenter, built the red house where she and her five younger brothers and sisters were born. Her mother died when she was thirteen and the youngest child still a baby. She kept house for them all until all but one brother were grown and gone, and then she kept house for her father and brother. For the last twenty years, since her father and then her brother died, she has been alone.

Most of this we learned later and almost incidentally. What a bleak and meager life its summary suggests. No husband or children, no paid occupation, little education, few journeys, hardly any money, solitary old age. And yet, it is a life that Miss Mount perceives as crowded with vivid events and memorable experiences, and rich with possibility still. Some say, Oh, Ada Mount, how she goes on. But they say it smilingly. They like talking with her when they have time. Everyone does. She can take the commonplace stuff of anyone's life and make it shine.

She told us that first afternoon about the bear that chased her father up a tree and kept him there all one morning. About the sweet peas Mrs. Willard used to grow and walk into town to sell; her sweet peas were famous. About the great-nephew who left town with the circus the summer before last; left his wife and children and hasn't been heard from since. About lightning striking her church ten years ago, and it burned to the ground. But they soon raised the money to rebuild it! About how to make elderberry wine. About the fox who kept looking in her windows one winter, standing on the snowbank. About Ted Putnam's heifer winning first prize at the fair when Ted was just a little boy. About the night when someone stole half the Howletts' hens. Imagine the audacity of it! About Mr. Burton giving a great big wedding reception for his daughter, but he still wouldn't finish painting his house. Ha! Ha! About nursing her sister Agnes through the flu in 1918; she nearly died, but she didn't. About the great-great-niece who is at the university studying to be a veterinarian; she always liked animals. About the time Perry LeBeau shot Betsy Putnam's pet crow, by mistake, of course; but Betsy was heartbroken and so was Perry. About the year the apple crop was lost when it snowed in May; snow on the apple blossoms—what a sight that was. About where to look for the little wild orchids. About—

But I realize she couldn't have told us so much on that one visit. She stayed only an hour. She is a pointed and precise storyteller, not garrulous. But we must have heard some of this later. And much more, far more in three years than I can remember, although I find I can remember easily when I start to think about her. We must have had a hundred conversations in the last three years. Often when I see her in her garden as I'm driving by, I stop to talk a few minutes. I call her up whenever we have news of visitors for her column. Sometimes, not often, she walks up our hill again and stays a little while if she sees we're not busy. Several times she has asked us into her house, to show us something, a photograph, a carving, a bird's nest, some possession among a neat, crowded store of things of little apparent value that she cherishes, transfigures by telling about.

We will never be much more intimate than this, I suppose. She is truly close, we see, with the neighbors longest on the road, with several attentive nephews and nieces and their children, with church friends. But I gather that she finds our relations acceptable if only because we often hear from some other neighbor a version of something we have told her. About our discovering a stand of wood lilies. About the car full of rowdy boys who drove around our fields one summer night. About the hunter's bullet we dug out of the barn door. About the abandoned cat we found and the Howletts took in. About—I wish I could overhear her retelling these events, relishing them, filling them with her own sense of their interest and meaning.

I wish I could tell Miss Mount, without seeming to assume a greater closeness than we have, how we value her acceptance of us. We draw strength from her profound attachment to life. There is no place in her presence for discontent and drooping hopes. In her presence, we feel capable of ardent, avid response to the world.

Because I have never known anyone like Miss Mount, I can connect her only with this particular place, this quiet mile of country road which, in certain ways, has scarcely changed since she was born here. That must be one of the sources of her strength, this sense, this illusion, at least, of continuity. The ice storm that turns the trees to glass, the cow that has twins, the child with a new puppy: such events, on which her spirit first was fed, still nourish it. And yet, the changes here have been great, the irresistible changes in the way people live, even here, and especially in their hopes and fears for their children. And so I can only connect Miss Mount with a distant time and a vanished possibility.

To take what the gods have given, when they have given *nothing*, judged by standards so greatly changed, and to make of this *nothing* what Miss Mount makes of it: no, it's no longer a possibility. And yet . . . there are children on this road—Betsy, Perry—to whom the changes are not everything, not yet, as least, children who still live part of their lives as if in that distant time. Of course, they take Miss Mount for granted; she has always been there. But they owe her something.

Nearest Neighbors

꤮ Our earliest encounters with our near neighbors made us realize that, no matter how we chose to conduct ourselves, we belonged to this neighborhood. No matter whether we were friendly or aloof, became involved or went our own way, our presence would be noticed, talked about, felt. No matter what else we had in common, we were joined to others just by our presence in a particular place.

Little or nothing in our city life had prepared us for this sense of connection with strangers, and we could only guess, at first, at how we should proceed. We had the simplest kind of newcomer's wish to be on good terms with everyone, but little idea of what this might entail. Most of what we first knew or observed of our neighbors' lives only made us more conscious of how different our own had been. We took it for granted that the differences went deep.

We knew that Mr. Howlett had recently retired after thirty years as Whitcomb's town clerk. That Mr. LeBeau was a machinist with one of the plants. That Ted Putnam was a draftsman at another. That his widowed mother, Elizabeth Putnam, who lived across the road from Ted and his family, had been a nurse. That Mr. Burton, among other occupations dependent on his battered truck, was our local trash man; and that Mrs. Burton clerked at Sears, Roebuck. We saw that all the men were farming as well, if only with a cow or two and a fattening steer and a flock of chickens. Each barnyard held its testimonial tractor and manure pile. Every open, level hay-field was mowed, every hilly pasture grazed. Most mornings we could faintly hear the Howletts' rooster crowing.

We could see, or felt, that what we had done with the Willard place must strike our nearest neighbors as just what rich city people would do. In the city we were anonymous enough among the shifting ranks of the relatively prosperous. In the country we were suddenly visible as the new people in the big house on the hill. I feared not dislike, nor even envy or resentment, but something closer to disapproval, an impersonal kind of disapproval, but a separating feeling still. Nine rooms for two people and a lawn like velvet. Where was the justice in that, and didn't we know that the common lot was hard work and scarcity? I suppose I felt that the men who worked on the house were disapproving in this way, and so we could never truly be friends, for this if for no other reason.

And other reasons might abound with these neighbors. What, for instance, would we find to talk about? I suppose this was a question three years ago. Now I can smile at my ignorance. But then, at first, it was hard to conceive even of the circumstances in which conversation might begin, although I was sure, if Gil wasn't, that it must begin somehow. Miss Mount's first call convinced me of that, made me impatient for it even, although she was clearly incomparable. But her call was a beginning, and I hoped she'd given a good report of us.

One Saturday not long after he'd come to offer us his help in getting settled, we saw Ted Putnam at his mailbox as we were driving to town. We stopped and thanked him again for his kind intention and said we seemed to be managing all right so far. Then a thin, fair-haired girl of nine or ten came up and was introduced, and that was Betsy, his elder daughter. And the other was Carrie, he said, the younger one over there playing with the beagle, and in a minute or two Nancy Putnam came out of the house. She's been wanting to meet us, she said, and we stayed for a few minutes more talking. Except for Betsy. She simply stared, looking intensely interested, like Miss Mount, a promising look, I thought. So then we knew the whole Ted Putnam family. I don't remember what we talked about, but, after three years of conversation here, I can guess.

We had seen Elizabeth Putnam a number of times on the

road walking her black dog, the tall, straight, white-haired woman managing with remarkable dignity to follow on a straining leash the frisky, smiling dog. It was impossible not to smile back at the dog, and one day when my smile spilled over onto Mrs. Putnam, she nodded and smiled. And the next day she was on the phone to say that she greatly appreciated the care we took in driving past Alfie because he was such a flibbertygibbet and even on the leash might make a reckless move. I told her how much we'd enjoyed meeting Ted and his family, and we talked for several minutes. I liked the sound of her voice, firm, vigorous, and somehow kind.

Encouraged to be a little daring, and on the strength of that remembered glance of hers, I called Mrs. Howlett to say, wouldn't she come back again, now that we were more or less settled and not at all busy, and let me show her the house. She came, and we took a tour, the first of many, because I realized, starting with Mrs. Howlett, that of course people who had always known the house were curious. Shyly praising our changes—the porches, the fireplaces, such a lovely kitchen—she surprised me by saying it didn't seem as different as she'd expected. Yes, this was where Mrs. Willard kept the broody hens, except we'd made one big bedroom out of two smaller ones; and here where we had a settee in the living room was just where the Willards' harmonium had stood. Her shyness brought out mine, but that in its way made us comfortable with each other, and we talked.

It didn't seem quite tactful to begin our acquaintance with Mr. Burton by asking him if he would come and get our trash, so Gil took it to the dump in the Blazer for the first few weeks, until the day in late October when Mr. Burton rattled up the hill in his truck, not to enlist us as customers, but to tell us he'd like to go on hunting in our woods and hoped we weren't going to post them. The way so many of the new people had. On Tom's advice, we didn't plan to post, and we told him so. Reassured, he sat down and accepted a glass of beer. We thought surely, from a certain convivial look to him, that he'd toss it off and accept another, but, on the contrary, he slowly sipped. A man who rushes nothing, he sipped, and we talked, and when at last his glass was nearly empty, we felt we knew him well enough to mention our trash. Yes, he thought he could fit us in, he said, as if the possibility had just occurred to him, as it probably had. And so we were incidentally able to make a necessary arrangement while having a good long talk.

It was only the LeBeaus, then, of our nearest neighbors, with whom we had still had no introductory exchange in those first weeks. Not even the smallest of the children waved to us. Well, *they* disapproved, I thought, the seven or eight of them packed into that small house with the hens eating up every blade of grass around it. Or was it because, they were French? They had a kind of dark, mistrustful *French* look, not that the LeBeaus, after generations here, were any more French than we were.

But for some reason, they were unapproachable, and perhaps always would be, we thought. Until the afternoon when my sheer city innocence made Mr. LeBeau smile. Driving down our road, I found it blocked by his cows, which he was herding up the road to the pasture that abuts our land. I stopped the car and jumped out for a better look at this charming rural scene, exclaiming in headlong enthusiasm to Mr. Le-Beau, Oh, aren't they lovely! The moment he was certain I really meant his animals, a sight as prosaic to him as his kitchen stove, he grinned. I had amused him and was glad. Glad of that not unfriendly grin, I asked an ignorant question or two about the herd, and was answered. It was a beginning. The LeBeaus, even Perry, are still the hardest to talk to, but we talk.

Our subject matter? The weather and the crops, of

course—the immemorial topics of most of the human race. The weather literally, because it's a matter of interest and concern, an experience of pleasure or dismay, each day all year long. Wasn't that a terrible thunderstorm. Is it ever going to rain. Will it ever stop raining. It feels like snow, doesn't it. Well, we're due for some snow. What a perfect evening. Partly, this weather talk is just friendly sound, but it's important to us all, too, the weather. It determines much of what we see every day and some of what we do. Willy-nilly, we perceive its every change, in the darkening morning or the clearing afternoon, in the fields turning brown in dry October, greening up again in a rainy April. The weatherman predicts, and we all attend, trade forecasts back and forth, but most of the time we're just as glad to be surprised, to have a sense of taking part, all as equals, in a mystery.

But of course it was a shame not to know that cloudburst was coming to spoil Mr. Howlett's hay. Yes, he'd just cut his back field that morning, and now it's only fit for bedding; too bad, isn't it. And there we are, turning naturally from the weather to our other subject, the crops. According to season, is the sap running yet, how is the hay coming or the corn ripening, are the tomatoes almost ready to pick. And we have hay, although it's the Austins who take it, and we cut firewood and have sold timber, and we pick our apples and wild blueberries, though not very diligently; but still we can keep our end up in the crop talk, for it's amazing how much there is to say about one hayfield if you really get to know it.

But I don't mean that we just go on and on about the literal crops. There's the rest of the yield of life, its precious surplus of rewards and recognitions, acquisitions and accomplishments, beyond the full hay-mow or freezer replete with beans. There's the new grandchild, the new chain saw, the trip to Burlington, the visit to the carnival, the blue ribbon for the afghan, the student who's made the honor roll, the fresh paint on the barn, the black cat's white kitten, the eagle scout's picture in the paper, and always the birthdays and holidays to be celebrated unstintingly, if only for the pleasure of the young. It's the young we talk most about, after the hay, their progress toward prospects unknown to any previous generation, or so it seems. And I talk about my stepson, Steve, and my brother's children, or about Betsy with her grandmother, or about Perry with Mrs. Howlett, who's raised four boys and all of them turned out pretty well so far, thank goodness.

The weather and the crops—that's what we talk about. And occasionally about our small misadventures—the chimney fire, safely extinguished; the car in the snowbank, rescued almost intact; the child thrown from a horse, but only shaken up, not hurt. Yes, this is usually the closest we come to talking about real trouble. There's Mrs. LeBeau's old father who's up in Hanover dying of cancer; and we feel for Mrs. LeBeau, but what is to be said about why her father goes on suffering. And there's Mrs. Burton's sister who stays with the Burtons when she's not in the mental hospital and wanders up and down the road like a poor lost soul. But the Burtons are good to her, and we all are used to her and make her welcome as best we can when she appears in our yards. And maybe one of the Howlett boys hasn't turned out so well after all, but no one seems to know where he is or what may be the matter. And none of this is *daily* life. Perhaps, behind the closed doors at night, there is anger and grief and dread that has never been revealed to us in three years, but I don't think so. What amazes me is the refusal to curse the bread or want to change places with anybody. What amazes me is the sense of contentment with so many things as they are that lights up the faces and puts some gaiety into the voices as we pass the time of day.

And I don't think we have disturbed that sense of contentment by exciting more than passing disapproval. Since we got the house and grounds done over, our neighbors can see we haven't spent much on the place, and surely rich people wouldn't leave a barn in the state ours is in, and Gil doesn't even own a tractor, something he would dearly love to have. We go to New York from time to time and we have a house full of books, but Elizabeth Putnam gets to California every year to visit her daughter, and Mrs. Howlett paints, and Mr. LeBeau has a snowmobile, and Ted Putnam collects tropical fish—such are some of the other natural disparities among us. Mr. Burton, at his leisure, as he loads our trash, can tell how much whiskey we drink, but he owns almost as much land as we do, and the LeBeaus own more. So I remind myself in an effort to refrain from punishing myself with guilt for having what I clearly don't intend to give up. Mr. LeBeau plows the snow from our driveway for us, and Perry has been my mainstay in the garden, but otherwise we are quite self-reliant. Properly so, for certainly it is better to be able to do for ourselves at least some of the work our neighbors do. They know far more that is of consequence to us than we know of much use to them.

And so we don't believe that any of them regard us as intruders. They have shown us nothing but friendliness and kindliness. We have a few other, perhaps closer, certainly different personal ties here, but none that mean more to us, day by day. The passing conversations in the road, the chance encounters working or walking in the woods, the casual, occasional visiting back and forth, usually when there's some small errand to accomplish, eggs to buy, squash to be given away, a birthday present to deliver to a child, a catalogue to share, a tool to be returned, a new calf or new rose bush to be seen: it's not daily, any of it, especially not in winter, but nothing else human involves us so continuously and convincingly with this place.

63

Are we truly friends, then, friends who might expect to be able to put our friendship to a considerable test? Elizabeth Putnam is such a friend, I believe; and so, in a way, different because they are children still, are Betsy and Perry. Three true friends, at least, and nothing but friendliness among the rest, among people who were strangers three years ago but who were then, no less than now, *neighbors*, a connection we begin to understand.

Neighbors Up the Road

ᔥ It seems that we hardly considered beforehand the extent to which the happiness of our country life might depend on other people. Or we considered it, in a sense, by a process of exclusion, by shunning the more obvious haunts of people like ourselves. Adam and Eve, Crusoe and Friday, the pioneer couple in their clearing: some bright, fanciful image of shared solitude had drawn us on farther and farther from the city. We hadn't been unsociable there, and yet we hardly considered the possibility of wanting or needing to make friends in the country. We didn't expect to be lonely. We intended to have visitors. It hadn't occurred to us to consider the kind of welcome that people in the country might care to offer strangers.

When we first saw those handsome houses on the more prosperous stretch of the road, we had thought that someday, since they weren't far away, we might get to know some of their inhabitants, but it seemed a remote eventuality. And then we encountered the Talcotts on our lawn, and a few days later we found in the mail a card from them asking us to a cocktail party the following week. We were surprised, pleasantly so, and momentarily disconcerted by our sense of pleasure. Why should we be glad to find, in our rural mailbox, this citified invitation?

But of course we were feeling drastically uprooted then. We were suddenly, vividly conscious of the degree to which we had cut ourselves off from every familiar resource. It was exhilarating, I remember, this feeling that we would have to build our world anew, but we had begun to realize that of course there would be people in it. There was Miss Mount, coming to call, and perhaps some of them would be people not unlike ourselves after all, for there were the Talcotts on the lawn. We were finally beginning to appraise truly our taste and fitness for solitude, and it seemed that it might be pleasant to go to a party.

I remember that party very well. The Talcotts greeted us with unmistakable warmth, told us that everyone was eager to meet us, and began a round of introductions that seemed to confirm this statement. We smiled, bowed, shook hands, trying to catch the names, hearing on all sides kindly words of welcome and generous wishes for the happiness of our new life. Basking in their cordiality, we liked everyone we met, the doctor, the lawyer, the retired stockbroker, the chief of one of the local plants, and their wives. And not to our regret, since, of course, it made them seem so congenial, they seemed inevitably to be people much like ourselves, even to the fact that most of them had originally come from someplace else. All the men except Gil were in tweeds and all the women except me were wearing long skirts, but we could easily adopt such dress. We saw that the Talcott's living room was much like our own. We had a fine time and went home convinced that by sheer good luck our lack of forethought in the matter of friendship wasn't going to present difficulties.

More coolly in the next few days, we reappraised the gathering. Who were all those agreeable people, which of them were from New York, and what was it that they did here; and had we come all this way to involve ourselves in this apparently most conventional kind of social life; but perhaps we would never hear from any of them in any case, and, oh dear, that might be too bad after all, for they certainly had nice manners. I called the Talcotts with our thanks, and we thought about asking them to dinner as soon as we were a little more settled, but then Eleanor Gray, whom we remembered meeting at the party, called and invited us to dinner. Charles and Margery Forster, whom we'd also met, were there, and we had such a pleasant evening and felt so much at home with the Grays and the Forsters, like the Talcotts, our neighbors up the road, that we came away certain again of our good fortune.

Nothing that has happened since has changed that feeling. We see some of the people from that first party only occasionally, at the occasional party of similar size to which we are asked, but especially among the neighbors who were are the party, we found that those first expressions of friendliness were truly meant. Perhaps it was all more tentative at first than I can recall, and perhaps it might have worked out differently, but what I remember now is how natural it seemed that these neighbors should become friends.

There is that simple territorial bond, so surprising to us in its strength, not so strong as with our nearest neighbors, but still a constant source of mutual interest. There is the fact that newcomers are a rarity, too insignificant in number to seem a threat to the accustomed order of things, so rare as to be attractively novel to people who haven't gotten tired of each other but haven't had a surfeit of new aquaintances. And then the friendliness of these neighbors is so undemanding that to extend it to newcomers imposes little strain on either side. Most of our entertainments are simple enough, the impromptu supper or gathering for drinks, the outings arranged to see the beaver pond or drive up the mountain, to go to the art show or the summer theater.

Most of our conversation is effortless, familiar. We talk about the events of the day revealed to us by the *Times* and the television news, about local happenings we know of from the *Sentinel* or our own involvement, about our reading or our travels. And yet even though none of us farms, we have our weather and crop talk, too. Our experience of nature is direct and intense, stirring to us in ways that we share.

George Gray, the retired banker, mows his own fields, riding his tractor all day under the hot sun. John Talcott, the former professor of chemistry, is rapt with pleasure at the sight of the snowy cauliflower or the satiny eggplant he has just gathered from his garden. Margery Forster, picking black-berries, is entranced by their ripe scent and hardly feels the scratches the briers are inflicting. Gil and I are standing under a tree laden with apples, trying to shake some of the fruit down and catch it as it falls. We are clumsy and we laugh at our own awkwardness and in delight, and Eleanor Gray, whom we happen to tell, laughs in the same way. John Talcott gives much of his harvest away and receives in return for the flawless eggplant or cauliflower our heartfelt admiration of them. And at Christmas we savor a jar of Margery Forster's jam, remembering what she said about the fragrant berries and the sharp thorns. And we see George Gray getting off his tractor at last and stop to say, how wonderful your fields look and doesn't the grass smell sweet. And almost always we greet each other with a comment on the weather, and almost always, except on the meanest day, with words that celebrate the slant of the light, the wildness of the wind, the calm of the falling snow, the cold of dawn, the heat of midday, the darkness of the night.

Yes, the loveliness around all of us here is common ground. And yet the perception of it is different up and down the road. George Gray lets the grass lie in the fields, so what

67

can a summer hailstorm matter to him, but Mr. LeBeau's cows will need hay all winter. John Talcott rejoices when the early frost spares his garden, but not in the same way as Mrs. Howlett, who was *counting* on another week or two of picking and preserving. Perhaps those extra jars of tomatoes won't really make much difference to the Howletts' comfort, and Mr. LeBeau may be hardly breaking even with his cows in any case, if he gives a fair value to his time. But it's the sense of things that counts.

Down the road, our neighbors still connect the weather and the land with work and its fruits. Up the road, the connection is closer to the spirit of play, to spontaneous discovery and pleasure freely bestowed. The people up the road have never felt dependent on the land. Down the road, they still do, if only out of stubborn, loving habit. It's not a hard and fast distinction, but it's a difference. Some of the time, at least, we sing nature's praises for different reasons.

Elizabeth Putnam is on friendly terms with our neighbors up the road and, if she chose to, might see them more often than she does. She always goes to the Grays' big New Year's Day party, and so do the Howletts, but that is almost the only private social occasion when the two halves of our neighborhood meet. Thinking with persistent regret of that party we didn't give for the men who worked on our house, I sometimes fantasize a gathering of everyone we care for up and down the road. To the extent that I feel our nearest neighbors have accepted us as friends, I am troubled by the knowledge that almost certainly I will never have such a gathering. To the extent that we have discovered that the differences don't run so deep, I feel a disloyalty to our nearest neighbors in thinking that such a gathering would seem like an artificial occasion to everyone. No one would truly enjoy it, I suppose, except perhaps Miss Mount. Some of the differences do run deep, and some of the least important differences would seem the most awkward, and only a child could imagine one party making a happy family of the human race.

It doesn't occur to me to ask myself whether a neighbor up the road is my *true* friend because I think our notions of friendship are more or less the same. If we feel closer to our friends up the road, it is only because we are all sufficiently alike in ways that make friendship easy. *If* we feel closer. I feel close even to Mrs. Burton's wandering sister for reasons that have something to do with the differences between us. I feel close to all our nearest neighbors to some degree just because we may have to make a certain effort, each of us, to understand one another. It is pleasant not to worry that our friends up the road might disapprove of our prosperity, but why should they. It is touching that our nearest neighbors never seem to have disapproved, as well they might.

But how lovely, how amazingly lucky it seems to have so much friendliness from two different worlds. To laugh in the same day at Charles Forster's ironic appreciation of the *Times'* lead editorial and Mr. Howlett's amused, admiring account of what a racy bird with the hens his old rooster Bill still is. To be asked in the same week to come and see Betsy Putnam's new lot of baby chicks and to meet the Grays' visitors from Rome. I wouldn't like to try to weigh the relative pleasure of these happenings. Good luck gave us both, and we are dependent on them now. They are as necessary to our happiness as solitude.

Whitcomb

ༀ The old photographs show that Whitcomb once was a town of considerable charm, when Main Street was lined with elms, and churches and houses stood at pleasant intervals along it in the midst of shady lawns. The elms were probably doomed in any event, but long before the Dutch elm disease began to ravage New England they were sacrificed to the needs of the automobile and notions of progress and prosperity that were common enough elsewhere but not so common in Vermont. Main Street was widened and paved and curbs and sidewalks built. The churches and houses lost their front lawns, and the side lawns were lost to new commercial buildings and parking lots. The houses and most of the commercial buildings were allowed to age with little grace. And so that rather charming old street the photographs show was transformed into the earnestly utilitarian thoroughfare that we are familiar with but are still surprised to know so well and with such a sense of attachment.

We had thought wistfully, while we were still in the city, of picturebook villages we had seen and regretfully of Whitcomb. It seemed a pity that the Willard place was near such a workaday town. Tom Sargent and Clara Willard and Mr. Tyson and, in fact, everyone we met except Paul Channing seemed to like the town pretty well, but except for Paul none of them had ever lived anywhere else. Whitcomb had proved useful while we needed carpenters and plumbers and electricians, but once we were settled we expected to have little to do with it. We were moving to the *country*, not to a small town. The poets and novelists we had read were never lyrical about small towns.

In small ways, at first, Whitcomb began to disarm us, not by making any effort to do so but simply by continuing to accommodate us. During the first month after our move, we shopped in almost every store in town for small necessities for the house and were rarely disappointed. I liked the supermarkets and found everything I wanted in them. Gil saw a dentist, and we both had haircuts. I had some picture framing done and Gil got his watch cleaned. I remember very well the day in the first month when we were on our way into town for the ninth or tenth time and I thought, and said to Gil, imagine what it would be like if we were near one of those picturebook villages. In the simplest way, which we had failed to anticipate, we had already begun to rely on Whitcomb.

It hadn't occurred to us that a town of ten thousand people could do so many things. As we learned in our first months, it would be possible to depend entirely on Whitcomb, starting out, as Betsy Putnam did, with the attentions of a local obstetrician in the local hospital, ending, as Mr. Willard did, at the nursing home, the undertaker's, and the lovely old hilltop cemetery. You can't buy a mink coat or acquire an advanced degree or have open-heart surgery or expect to hear Rostropovich play in the local concert series, but it is easier to name such limitations as these than to account even briefly for all the town's capabilities. Perhaps that vision of decades ago that required the sacrifice of the elms was more ambitious than the present reality, but the reality is a town that appears to offer most of what ten thousand people need and desire. They go elsewhere to have an outing, a change of scene, but not often just because what they want or need is unobtainable in Whitcomb.

The novelists must have persuaded us that a small town is a simple place, easy to know and understand, easy to judge in unequivocal and almost certainly unflattering terms. We were ready to scorn Whitcomb; it is easy to scorn this drab-looking town. And yet now we see even its appearance as a matter too complex for simple judgment.

Whitcomb renounced its nineteenth-century charm in order to become, in a small way at least, a modern manufacturing town. What a pity, the scornful observer will say at the sight of the factory buildings lined up on the way into town. But the truth is more complex.

The truth seems to be that the plants enabled the town

to preserve its essential character and save itself from certain fates far less remediable than drabness. It is not a dying picturebook village nor a resort town in thrall to the tastes of city people. It has grown steadily, but slowly enough not to be overwhelmed by change. It had prospered modestly, but remains essentially as it was, a country town surrounded by farmland, not because farming thrives but because of the plants. Families have been able to hold onto land and pay the doctor and the car dealer, the music teacher and the bookstore proprietor, because of the jobs available in the plants. Farming has declined here for complex reasons, but a five-minute drive from the center of town most of the farmland is still intact.

The plants employ nearly three thousand men and women, not all of them from Whitcomb. The pay is decent, and most of the work is skilled. The appearance of the plants is uninviting, but they give off neither noise nor fumes. They are the town's largest taxpayer. Perhaps the original vision that brought them here was grander, but they have grown and prospered over the decades without seeming to overwhelm Whitcomb. They are not celebrated here; they are simply taken for granted. But Whitcomb is modestly renowned, it so happens, for the machinery they produce, which is sold around the world.

But the truth is too complex for summary. Each of these factual statements is inadequate in some respect. Each could be qualified or elaborated on from Mr. LeBeau's experience or the Putnams' or Harry Goodwin's or the Willard family's or Mrs. Perkins's. We know too much or too little now to make the simplest generalizations confidently. And yet we go on being tempted to try to see this relatively small world whole.

Not just Tom and Clara and Mr. Tyson, and not just the people who have never lived anywhere else, but almost everyone we have met in four years seems to like the town pretty well. Controversy abounds, over the size of the current school budget, the paving of a road, the latest decision of the zoning board, or almost any change in the familiar order of things. Most people are far quicker to find fault with the town than to praise it and take care to understate even their most favorable sentiments. And yet most people seem to feel a considered and specific kind of contentment with their lives here, for good reason.

It is only some of the young who say, challengingly, that they are discontented—boys, most of them, just finishing or just out of school. We see them idling around the shopping center, these restless boys, and read in the *Sentinel* about the disturbances they cause on Saturday nights. They say, as such boys say everywhere, that there is nothing for them to *do* in Whitcomb. Boy or girl, I can imagine feeling as they do—restless, curious, hungry for fresh experience. And yet I can't imagine for any except a few of them more promising lives elsewhere, wherever it might be.

I don't know of a better place to be a child or to raise children. I would infinitely prefer to grow old here rather than in the city or suburbs. I would rather be here if I were poor. I would rather be here if I were ill or mad or especially dependent in any way on the kindness and care of strangers. And yet I see those discontented boys at the shopping center and feel I might be among them. And yet I hope most of them will choose to stay. Even here, no one any longer *expects* the young to stay put. Except perhaps in a few farm families still, no child needs to be the one who never got away. Some of the most capable and curious must go away, and some of the least capable will drift away, and some of the girls, as girls do, will marry away. But I can't imagine for most who stay lives lived somewhere else with fewer constraints or more generous possibilities.

Whitcomb is small enough still for intimacy but large

enough for privacy. That part of its character which is busy, purposeful, sociable, that part which is so easy to mock, is faithfully represented in the *Sentinel*. But that part weighs lightly enough in most people's lives. You can take it or leave it and go your own way so long as the countryside is so generous still with the possibilities of solitude and self-reliance. The restless young must gradually discover their capacity for solitude and self-reliance. Yet I wouldn't care to mock the sociable occasions, the Memorial Day parade, the high school band concert, the church fair, the Christmas tree lighting, occasions filled with a kind of innocent pleasure I never thought to see.

Innocent. That isn't exactly the word I mean. I mean a feeling that is fresh and open and unalloyed, a feeling I scarcely associate with contemporary life. This spring I went to the garden club tea with Margery Forster. Fifty women were there, in bright spring dresses, talking and smiling with every evidence of pleasure. We heard some music, flute duets, a little Mozart, a little Handel, sweetly played by two pretty high school girls. We listened appreciatively and applauded warmly. We had our tea and ate our fill of nice little cookies and cakes, talking again, about the music and the weather and our gardens, smiling all the while, beaming at each other like pleased children, with unconcealed, wholehearted pleasure. I smiled, beamed, thinking with astonishment of how this occasion might belong to some time in the distant, perhaps more innocent past.

The older people we know here, Miss Mount, the Howletts, Elizabeth Putnam, feel that Whitcomb has changed so greatly in their lifetimes that they can hardly imagine what it will be like in the future. We have been struck by the town's resistance to change, by the stubborn integrity of its particular character in the face of all the pressures and temptations to submit to change. And yet we share the sense of uncertainty about the future that older people express. Not one of the plants is locally owned any longer. A year ago, the *Sentinel* was sold by its Whitcomb proprietor to a syndicate of small-town newspapers. Last spring a restaurant chain opened one of its garish outposts here. Our town government trades some degree of independence for large amounts of federal money. Sometimes we fear that the town is living out the last days of some older time, living on little more than the illusions of an almost bygone era. And when we ourselves feel this kind of uneasiness, we smile and shake our heads with a surprised sense of our attachment.

Our own dependence on Whitcomb still doesn't go very deep, if only because we don't depend on the town for our livelihood. The larger part of our attachment to the town is vicarious, derived from our sense of why most people like it here. But if we came here almost despite the town, we are glad to be here now in some personal way because of it.

Anyone who knows Whitcomb would laugh if I became lyrical about it. The shortcomings of its appearance are unarguable. But in this respect we have already seen certain changes for the better: a derelict house demolished, a shabby-looking store spruced up, a little park created in the middle of town. It happens slowly, as if there were plenty of time. Several young locusts have been planted on Main Street, mere saplings that won't be great trees for decades. But even now, at midsummer, their feathery green is promising, a statement of hopeful intent for the long future. And in the meantime, the garden club decks the street with flower boxes, brave strokes of color on a midsummer day, geraniums and marigolds defying the drabness. It's a hopeful gesture, at least, and a loyal one. It makes an impression. I smile at the sight of those flowers, suddenly feeling charmed by Main Street and unexpectedly fond of this nice town.

Elizabeth Putnam

❧ The most watchful and unsparing critic of Whitcomb we know is Elizabeth Putnam. Little that happens of importance in town escapes her notice or some measure of her disapproval. I like to see her when she is aroused. She is informed, specific, and as passionate in her indignation as someone can be only from the deepest feelings of attachment.

She and I began to get to know each other on account of, or at least in connection with, this sense of personal concern of hers. Soon after she called us the first time, about Alfie, she called again to say that, as neighbors, she thought we would be interested in the problem of the water supply for the trailer park. It was a bad situation. She was sending around a petition to the selectmen and hoped we might care to put our names on it. I asked if I might come by at the end of the afternoon, and she said that would be fine, and so I found myself, about five that day, being welcomed for the first time into the crowded, comfortable living room where I have since spent so many enjoyable hours. We were Mrs. Putnam and Mrs. Lovell that afternoon and through several more encounters, in the pleasant old way, but it was clear to both of us, I believe, that we would be friends. She offered me a cup of tea, and I said she shouldn't bother, and she said, well, how about a drink, that's no bother, and so in a few moments we were settled, drinks in hand, in the well-worn easy chairs the looks and feel of which are now so familiar to me.

I don't remember the details of the trailer park water problem, although Elizabeth explained them to me carefully and, at first, calmly. Of course, I didn't realize then that she was making a determined effort at restraint. The nub of the matter was that the trailer park must not be allowed to expand until the water problem was corrected. I couldn't help being interested as Elizabeth warmed to the subject and found it

76

irresistible as her calm disappeared and her ire rose and she began to remark in the most scathing terms on the greed of the trailer park owner, the incompetence of the health authorities, and the sloth and indifference of the selectmen.

I was fascinated, charmed, by my first exposure to this ardent nature. For several minutes, she continued at high intensity, until finally, after pausing as if to catch her breath for a fresh assault, she burst out laughing instead and said, oh, dear, Mrs. Lovell, you must think I'm a crotchety old soul to get so worked up, mountains out of molehills, you must be thinking, and the doctors say I mustn't get excited, but I can't help it, I tell them, and I suppose I enjoy it, you'll see, I'm an old warhorse. And she laughed again at her own caricature, so disarmingly that I began to laugh, and there we were, on that first afternoon, giggling like schoolgirls.

We got down to business again, and I said that of course Gil and I would sign the petition, and just then Betsy came to the door and came inside to let her grandmother know, she said, that her father would be over after supper to fix the leaky faucet. When I smiled and said hello she murmured a greeting. But there was nothing diffident about the way she glanced at me, and I even thought, a promising thought, that it might have been my presence that had brought her over just then. But after a brief exchange with her grandmother, she was off again.

And Elizabeth said, I'm sure that child came over just to have another look at you, she's dying of curiosity. I said something about what a nice little girl she seemed to be, and that set Elizabeth off in a way that, already, I seemed to recognize. Oh, yes, there was nothing wrong with Betsy; she was smart as a whip and nice as she could be most of the time, but her manners were atrocious, bursting in and bursting out that way, without a proper how-do-you-do for a guest, and going on ten, old enough to know better, not her parents' fault, but. . . The tone was familiar. I thought of the trailer park water problem and smiled. And Elizabeth understood at once, paused, and laughed. Well, you can see, she said, that I don't take things lightly, and that child is the apple of my eye, so I want her to be *perfect*. And I suppose, she said, that I expect too much.

We went on talking a while longer, longer than I realized until I finally looked at my watch. We were talking casually about this and that, unexceptionable neighborhood matters mostly, as I recall, shifting naturally from one subject to the next as if we were already friends accustomed to this kind of effortless, unhurried exchange. We were both surprised when we found how late it had become. Where did the time go, one of us said; and we smiled at each other in pleased agreement on the way it had gone. We said good-by without making another plan to meet but knowing that we would certainly be seeing each other again soon.

We have spent countless hours together or in conversation on the telephone since that first afternoon. There is no one in Whitcomb I would rather talk to and no one else I count on in the same way. We are unlikely friends on the face of it and are charmed partly by novelty. But I am not truly strange to her experience, while she is altogether fresh in mine, and so is our friendship, a country friendship.

Whenever it seems to me that I have known someone like Elizabeth before, I realize that what has come to mind is not the memory of any real person in my life but a kind of mythical woman of an earlier day whose image I fashioned long ago from family reminiscence, old photographs, childhood reading. In ways that seemed denied by modern life, if only by its physical ease, this mythical woman was always an exemplary figure to me. Whatever her role, she was called upon to chance the unknown, brave danger, endure hardship and privation, overcome grave obstacles and difficulties. Whatever goals she set herself, she labored without stint and without vanity. She was driven, perhaps, by her sense of purpose, but she was free of petty ambitions and cares and of futile, dispiriting doubt. She was free in spirit in a way that the elaborate imperatives and pervasive uncertainties of modern life had surely foreclosed.

How Elizabeth would laugh if I presented to her, as an alter ego, this superlatively virtuous creation of my young fancy. She would be purely amused by the idea of herself as any kind of heroine. But as time and place permitted, she has lived more of that independent and yet dedicated life I once romanticized than anyone else I have known. She herself sees her life as anything but romantic and is amused, but pleased too, I know, by the way I so often try to draw her out about it, especially when we have Betsy with us, a young listener for exemplary tales.

I sometimes have to remind myself that Elizabeth's history is hardly a generation longer than my own. It confuses me when she recalls making the rounds with her father, a doctor who practiced all his life in Whitcomb, and waiting in the buggy, holding the horse's reins, while he called on a patient. That was over half a century ago, in her childhood, but in modern life. And when she herself first began to work here as a nurse, she visited patients in the hills and hollows at the end of rough dirt roads on horseback or on foot. That was in the 1930's, my childhood, not so long ago. And in that same recent decade, when she married Will Putnam, they bought the only place they could afford, a farm long abandoned and so overgrown and tumbledown it was almost like homesteading to bring it back. There they were, cutting and clearing and fencing, not on the prairie a hundred years ago, but just forty years ago in Vermont. They plowed and planted and built up their dairy herd, and had two children, and made the rambling old farmhouse comfortable, and after a decade began to think life was going to be easier.

Then on a bitter cold and windy February night, Will

Putnam, as usual, stoked up the wood-burning furnace before they went to bed, and two hours later fire swept the house, and parents and children in their nightclothes fled into the snow. Firemen came, but by dawn there was nothing left of the house and its contents but a cellarhole full of ashes. That was thirty years ago, but country houses sometimes burn that way still. Yet when I read of these fires in the *Sentinel*, I wonder how many families now, faced by such losses, go on with their lives as the Putnams did. Their barn and animals were spared, so they still had their livelihood. There was a little insurance, and with a lot of their own labor they built the small house I know. By one means and another they acquired a stock of the daily necessities, clothes, dishes, beds, and they went on with their lives essentially as before, as if that devastating fire had been an incidental event that in no way lastingly disturbed or diminished their sense of the possibilities of the particular life they had chosen to lead. They farmed and Ted and his sister Anne grew up and a decade passed that Elizabeth remembers as very happy. She would never call it the happiest of her life, not caring for such distinctions, but perhaps it was.

Then, one summer evening while he and Ted were getting a load of hay into the barn, Will Putnam had a stroke, and a day later he was dead. Elizabeth wanted to keep the farm going, but it was time for Ted and then Anne to go away to college, and she never could find a dependable hired man, and after three years, the hardest perhaps of her life, she gave it up. I admitted defeat, she says, with a wry smile that fades into a thoughtful, puzzled look, as if she were still trying to figure out why the farming had been too much for her.

But the next fifteen years turned out to be as busy and, in certain ways, as satisfying as any that had gone before. She went back to school for a year, and then she went back into nursing, starting as a surgical nurse at the Whitcomb hospital, becoming head surgical nurse there, then going back to being a visiting nurse because she'd loved it, then becoming head nurse of the new convalescent center, and all the while involving herself more and more deeply in the community life of the town, especially anything to do with health, meaning almost anything at all affecting bodies and minds—sending children to summer camp, seeing that no family lacked winter fuel, finding the money to expand the birth control clinic, getting up a system for keeping in touch with the old living alone, persuading officialdom or the citizenry to support the endless succession of good causes. As I am aware from reading the *Sentinel*, most of this sort of work is done faithfully by a rather small number of people, and for years Elizabeth was one of them, all the while continuing an exacting professional life, keeping house, mothering her children as they still needed her. She says with a smile that sometimes she used to think that the farming had been easier.

And all of this was too much for her finally, after fifteen years, after a slight heart attack and then another more serious one. The year before we came here she was obliged to give up her job and most of the causes. I must want to live, she says, if I'm willing to live this way, the way the doctors tell me to. She gestures impatiently at the cramped space around her, the confining walls of the small living room in which the doctors would have her spend so much of her time. She doesn't look or seem ill. She speaks and gestures with youthful expressiveness. She sits straight in her chair and gets up from it decisively. She has drastically curtailed her life because she wants to go on living, but the spirit won't comply, won't subside, ardently protests its need to care and be concerned. About the trailer park water problem. About Betsy. About me.

It seems to me that Elizabeth could hardly have had the time for our friendship earlier in her life. In part, at least, I am a beneficiary of the surplus of time she has now. She still does what she can for the causes, mostly on the telephone. She sees her family across the road and goes out with old friends. Every spring she visits Anne in California. Every summer she plants and tends an inordinately large garden, refusing emphatically to curtail this fruitful rite. She reads and sews and looks after Alfie. But she always has, or says she has, time for me whenever I call her up or stop by. This is the country, she reminds me, and that is part of it, too, a state of mind shaped not by a surfeit of human contact but by its scarcity.

Often, by way of an excuse for a call or unannounced visit, I have some advice to seek. Especially during our first year, when we needed to make every kind of practical arrangement, Elizabeth was our great recourse. Perhaps it was flattering to her that we were forever asking her to recommend a doctor or mechanic, to tell us when to put on the snow tires or get the chimney cleaned, to tell us whether we needed lightning rods or how to keep deer out of the garden. But surely any questioner must be flattered by her response. She makes me feel that my least dilemma is interesting to her and worthy of scrupulous attention. She is simply incapable of indifference. For that very reason, I suppose, I might hesitate to make that serious test of our friendship that presently unimaginable circumstances might propose, but I don't think I would hesitate for long. She would turn first, I suppose, to her family across the road, just as we would if our families were near at hand. But our families are far away, and Elizabeth is near.

I usually think, when I am knocking at her door, that I'll only stay a few minutes, and then an hour passes. Sometimes she has a cause she wants to take up with me, not necessarily to enlist my support, but more often, as she says, just to relieve her feelings, knowing by now, certainly, how much I enjoy her wildest excursions into advocacy and scorn. If only I could *do* more, she says, I wouldn't talk this way.

But you lead me on, she says. And I do. Elizabeth speaks from years of the most intimate involvement with this town and its people. I am fascinated to learn some of what she knows. From the boards, committees, societies, the public and private seats of authority, from the doctors' waiting rooms and consulting rooms, the sickbeds, the deathbeds. Most of what I know about Whitcomb that lies beneath its calm surface I have learned from Elizabeth. The old and the new conflicts and enmities, the forgotten and the fresh scandals, and also the countless acts of tolerance and forebearance, of generosity and devotion. I have no illusions about this town, Elizabeth likes to say, but often as not in preamble to her tribute to some evidence of enlightenment, some good deed. While any current question is in doubt, she assumes the worst, at least for conversational purposes. At a satisfactory outcome she expresses astonishment. And yet she has persuaded me, through her own repeated testimony, that Whitcomb is worthy of her regard.

Betsy often comes over when I am visiting Elizabeth, making us a threesome of three generations, approximately, with a taste for one another's company. I am rarely conscious of our different ages, except that Betsy and I are inclined to defer to Elizabeth, not to her years but to the clearly superior interest of her experience.

She tells us about her life, not in the faintly false tone of legend or saga that I'm afraid I fall into but in down-to-earth and pointed episodes. Her contest with a stubborn but stupid bull. A ninety-year-old patient's courtship and proposal of marriage when she was first nursing and hardly more than a girl. The newborn baby left in her parked car on one of those dirt roads in the middle of nowhere. The ghost in the old farmhouse, not a ghost, of course, but loose boards in a hidden closet it took them a long while to find. The way Ted, when he was even younger than Betsy, found the water for a new well after the dowser had given up. The way Anne hid the calf on the day it was due to be butchered. And about the fire. Of course we want to hear about the fire, Betsy and I, such a terrible happening, worse in a way than a death, because death happens inevitably to everyone. But Elizabeth talks about it matter-of-factly, reduces its terror to manageable size, even makes us smile by telling us of raking through the ashes and finding her mother's diamond engagement ring, almost as good as new; so, you see, not everything was lost.

Knowing as I do the well-developed nature of Elizabeth's critical faculties, I have wondered sometimes whether or not she ever exercises them on me, if only in her thoughts. One day this summer I almost asked her. We were picking beans in that great garden of hers, filling grocery bags from the endless, hopeless abundance of the long rows of vines. We were picking fast because it had begun to rain, and the rain might have spoiled a few of those beans. I was picking as fast as I could but not half as fast as Elizabeth. With my bag at last brimming with beans and going limp in the rain, I said to her, I think I'll stop. She straightened up and looked at me and looked around at the rows of beans still waiting to be picked, and I could see she wasn't ready to stop, because we hadn't finished.

It seemed to be a small test of character. I was conscious for the first time of risking her disapproval and thought of how critical she could be of the people she cared most for. Now, I thought, I might ask her whether my various faults and failings could possibly have escaped her attention. Just then, my laden, sodden bag gave way, dumping half a bushel of beans at my feet. We both exclaimed, groaned, and began to laugh. The moment for my question passed, if it was the moment, as we stood laughing helplessly in the bean patch in the rain. I looked across the vines at this tall, white-haired, kind-faced woman, unknown to me three years ago, and now my *friend*, beyond any questioning.

Mrs. Perkins

❦ It was through Elizabeth that Mrs. Perkins entered our country life, to lighten and also to cloud my Thursday mornings.

Elizabeth needs Mrs. Perkins's help, but I have no such medical excuse. I enjoy or at least don't mind most kinds of physical work but will gladly pay someone else to help with the endless repetitions of vacuuming, dusting, mopping. There was always someone in the city willing to do these things for me, almost always some serious, kindly, middle-aged, southern-born black woman disposed by the imperatives of another time and place to come and clean house for me, as if willingly. I knew there were no such women in Whitcomb and arrived with the resigned expectation that no woman in this small town and rural setting, in famously egalitarian Vermont, would consent to do another able-bodied woman's housework.

But I should have realized that poor, poorly educated women, wherever they live, still have little choice. It's what you do if you're a woman and can't do anything else and need the money—cleaning. I might have gotten the Talcotts' Mrs. Stubbs or the Grays' Mrs. Carpenter. Thanks to Elizabeth, I have Mrs. Perkins. And most of the time I am thankful.

During one of the first of our regular midmorning chats over coffee, Mrs. Perkins and I discovered that we are within a few months of being the same age. I hope she doesn't brood over this fact, as I do. In the very difference in the way we look, I see too plainly the force of circumstance. We are two middle-aged white women of Yankee stock who have little or no physical resemblance. My hair, skin, teeth, flesh, all attest to a lifetime of no expense spared. Mrs. Perkins represents one local version of rural poverty, not the most common one of pale obesity, but the rarer one of sallow leanness. In middle age, she is drab-haired and half toothless, all youthful comeliness gone.

A lifetime, generations, of hardscrabble want and need are expressed in Mrs. Perkins's looks, and in her ignorance. Much could be done, even now, to improve her appearance, but her ignorance of the world is daunting. Nine or ten years of schooling taught her to write and spell well enough and read what interests her in the *Sentinel*, mostly, for sufficient reason, the stories of fires and auto accidents. I have never known a city person as ill-informed as she is of whatever lies outside her own experience. Mrs. Addison, my last cleaning woman in New York, or Mr. Rivera, the porter in our apartment building, would think, mistakenly, that Mrs. Perkins is stupid. I have said that I would rather be poor in the country than in the city, but rural poverty can be more punishing in this respect, perhaps, in the starving of intellect.

Perhaps I am particularly struck by these bleaker aspects of Mrs. Perkins's being because of my sense that I have needed, to get through my life, every last nourishing meal and visit to the dentist, every hour of my long, expensive education, every moment of my reading. But I also see that Mrs. Perkins has gotten through her life with her self-respect intact and with qualities of character that seem almost unaccountably benign. Her manner is good-humored, her conversation good-natured. She is generous in her sympathies and loyal in her attachments. She loves the countryside, the trees and fields and weather, no less than I do. She is quite tenderly fond of dogs, cats, flowering plants, and small children. She

86

has a strength in the face of adversity that she has often had to call upon but draws from sources almost unimaginable in the childhood I now know something about.

Mrs. Perkins and I chat over coffee or bedmaking as if nothing of importance in our respective fates sets us apart. She happens to be a talkative woman, and much of the time, I have only to listen to the narratives which, in three years, have supplied me with her history. The meager childhood on the stonecrop farm, and the early marriage to the young man trying to farm another hundred hilly acres. The five children to raise somehow. The fire, like Elizabeth's, in the middle of a winter night, but with everything gone, house, barn, live-stock. They move into town, and her husband finds work at one of the plants, but he has started drinking. He has been drinking the night his car misses a curve on a back road. At least the children, all but the youngest girl, are grown and gone by then. Mrs. Perkins goes out to clean, comes to sit over coffee with me on Thursday mornings, and tells me about the fire or the fatal crash, about the farming years or the town years, calmly, without complaint, as if it were all commonplace, as if misfortune and hardship were too familiar to both of us to need comment.

Money has been scarce enough in this part of the world, and prosperity sufficiently discreet, to encourage the notion that we're all in the same boat. And a stubborn attachment to the principle that we were all created equal still sets the tone for most of the ways we get on with each other. Mrs. Perkins can keep her self-respect far more easily here, I think, than in the city. She doesn't seem to feel sorry for herself and would recoil from anyone else's pity. But I can't help feeling sorry for her children.

I have only met the youngest, Doris, a palely fat girl, gaps showing in her smile, at nineteen married and a mother, good-natured, ignorant. Mrs. Perkins dotes on her grandson and says Doris is a wonderful mother. Perhaps that little boy has more of a future than I think. There's much more help around for the asking than there was when Mrs. Perkins or Doris was growing up. Mrs. Perkins, with no apparent sacrifice of self-respect, has learned to claim whatever she is entitled to in the way of rent supplements, fuel allowances, legal advice, medical care. Perhaps Doris knows more than I guess about what a child needs, and knows where to turn to get it. A lot of it is there now. And what more does it take?

I have often asked Elizabeth this question. What does it take? To get a family out of the rut from one generation to the next. Just money? The Willards didn't have much more to do with than Mrs. Perkins's family, but none of the Willard children got stuck in a rut. The LeBeaus don't intend to let their children flounder. To love the trees and fields, to be good-natured and self-respecting isn't *enough*. Is it? For a whole life? I ask Elizabeth. She laughs, frowns, shakes her head, thinking of all the country people she has known, unable to reply.

Visitors

๛ We came here with few fixed expectations about the content of our country life, but one of them unmistakably entailed the presence of visitors. I remember our considering their comfort and convenience almost as attentively as our own while we planned the changes in the house. Counting the sofa in the sitting room that turns into a double bed and the four bunks in the room intended for children, we provided ten places for visitors to sleep. Ten! Almost the only change that Gil made in my furnishing plans was to call for a more expensive, presumably more comfortable, mattress for the sofa bed than the one I had chosen.

But this bed has never been used, and now I doubt that it ever will be. We have never had more than six visitors at once, and I don't believe we will ever exceed this number. When I think of all the cooking and all the talking, I can only hope we never will. We don't lightly invite visitors any longer, and visitors, for that matter, no longer have the same interest in coming. But when we were carefully making ready for ten we must have had something in mind, some grounds for making such a lavish estimate of our need and desire for company.

We had scarcely finished settling the house when we started having people to stay. Two couples, old friends from the city, were our first visitors, and I remember very well the satisfactions of the fine October weekend they were here. Except that we were unexpectedly weary at the end, I remember it as perfect—the house filled with gaiety, the fields and woods irresistibly inviting. Our friends' evident and expressed delight was perfect, exactly the response we must have been hoping for. We had evidently succeeded in providing great enjoyment to people we were very fond of. They, in turn, had given us various assurances we had hardly known we needed. That we had indeed acquired and created something lovely. That we hadn't, after all, cut ourselves off from every old and valued tie. That we would, in fact, be able to share some of the anticipated happiness of our country life with people we cared for, just as, judging by all those beds, we had intended to.

That weekend might not have gone so well if it had rained, if we had drunk too much, if anyone had seemed a little bored. It set a high standard, and yet we have found with friends, those first guests returning from time to time and others, that visitors continue to supply the same elements of pleasure. No friendship seems to have suffered so far from its country exposure, and one or two have been strengthened by the leisurely breakfasting, the now familiar walks, the idle hours of our rather frequent rainy afternoons. If we no longer invite friends, and they no longer come, as often as in the first year or so, it is not from disappointment.

I can't remember now exactly who our second visitors were, whether my father and stepmother or Gil's older brother and his wife. My albums are full of pictures of visitors, but not necessarily in proper sequence. I do remember feeling anxious beforehand, trying to reassure myself with the recollection of our friends' visit, and realizing that this one might be better or worse but couldn't be the same.

Both couples came at this time, within a weekend or two of each other, and now these initial family visits blur. My albums contain similar photos from both. There we are, we and our guests, sitting at the dinner table, starting out on a walk, posing for one another in front of the view. Everyone is smiling in these pictures, as they are in the snapshots recording the presence of other members of our families on later weekends as all our near relations came to see us. I study these three-year-old smiles now for meaning. They are not false smiles, and yet, I fear, they lack spontaneity. They are more expressive of good intentions than of irrepressible good spirits. I look at a dinner table scene from the first friends' visit, taken by Gil, and see that the friends and I in that moment of record are shaking with laughter. I have no idea now of what seemed so funny to us, but the remembered playfulness of that moment, verging on silliness, still makes me smile. In vain I search the family pictures for this look of innocent hilarity. I know that nothing untoward happened on those first two family visits, nor on the ones occurring, at growing intervals, since then. I don't have to search my memory to think of mealtimes, outings, conversations, with Gil's family and mine, that seemed particularly enjoyable.

And yet, for all the smiling faces of record and recollection, I am not satisfied.

On our sitting room mantel, beside the photograph of Mr. Willard, we have an enlargement of a snapshot, taken by Gil, of my brother's youngest child, David, when he was not quite four. He is swinging in our old swing in the maple. I had pushed him as high as he wanted to go, a good, daring height, and then stepped aside, and he is alone in the picture, caught by Gil's camera at the high point of the forward arc of the swing, a small, radiant figure in the sunlight filtered through leaves, swinging in the checkered shade, with a look on his face of perfect happiness. That picture is over two years old now and David, at six, is greatly changed. My brother and sister-in-law and the three children made several visits to us, but now they are living in the West, and heaven knows when they will get back here again. But that picture of David has lost none of its hold over me, its testimonial power, to some other viewer a charming picture of a smiling child, to me a vision still, but from real life, not just of a child's access to bliss but of the human genius for transcendance.

So, my hopes for our family visits are not impossibly high. Only that we might rise above rivalries and resentments, banish the spirit that sits in judgment and disapproves, pluck from our minds for a while the rooted sorrows of family life. I seem to want nothing less from us all in our country place, this earthly paradise where all should be joyful together. Naturally, the young have come closest—David and his sisters, and Steve, my stepson. I think Steve has been happy here. He usually brings a girl or two or three young people, and they roam around our land or go off to the lake to swim or the river to canoe, disappearing for most of the day, coming back for meals sunburned and hungry and still brimming with energy, laughing and joking with each other and with us, making these mealtimes as cheerful as any we have had in the country. Occasionally he comes by himself, and he and his father cut firewood or clear a stretch of one of the old logging roads, working contentedly together as they did when they were gathering the stones for the walls.

On such visits he seems very much *at home*. One of the bedrooms has always been called *Steve's room*. And yet others have occupied it more often than he has. The intervals between his visits grow longer. He is out of school now and at work in the city and evidently enjoying the first of his independent city life. It is quiet for him here, I suppose, compared to a young man's city, and it's a fair distance to come. We wish he would come more often but doubt that he will for a while. Perhaps, after all, he has never enjoyed himself here as much as I thought, hoped, he had. But when I see him in my mind's eye, a composite image of a young man with a steady gaze and artless smile, I dare to look to the future confidently. Someday Steve will marry and have children, and he and his family will come to stay with us, and I will push his child in the swing, and Gil will take that child's picture.

We had visitors every weekend from Memorial Day till Labor Day in our first summer and on several spring and fall weekends of that year. Every winter has been quieter, since, except for Steve, we have no skiers among our friends and relations. But in all of last year we had no more than a dozen rounds of guests; in this one, so far, not half a dozen. Curiosity has been satisfied, novelty lost. It's a fair distance to come. It must seem quiet here, I suppose, to most visitors. Our own needs for human contact have been satisfied increasingly near at hand, in the unlooked for friendliness and neighborliness of our country life. Perhaps our need for human contact has abated in the solitude of the country.

Certainly, the presence even of the dearest visitors no longer seems like a necessary culmination of our life but like a discontinuity, an interruption, however enjoyable, not just in routine, but in our closest ties with this place. No matter how sorry I feel to see visitors leave, sorry to think of how long it may be before we are together again, I also have a sense of integrity restored, not just to routine, but to the core of an experience which only the two of us who live here can hope to share.

The Birds

So long as there is daylight, we are almost never truly alone. Almost every moment of the day we can look out and see the birds, the only wild creatures that let themselves be observed so continuously, especially in exchange for food.

We have spent hundreds of hours, I suppose, just in watching from the house as the birds come and go at our feeders. It is easier to see them plainly and at length from inside the house, with the help of binoculars, for even though we have tamed them, in some sense, by drawing them to the feeders, we have only to open the door to send all but the chickadees flying as fast as they can for the treetops. And even though we see them so much of the time tamely pecking away at the seed and the suet, they are always vibrant with instinctual life. To be able to observe this life, hour after hour, is to have the means for trying to understand instinct itself. If the birds live purely by instinct, we ask, and yet with such astonishing complexity and intensity, what is *instinct* and what else do we live by? We read about the birds, of course, but we watch them as if we thought no one had ever done so before and we must inform ourselves entirely through our own observations.

I hardly like to think of how many hours I have spent watching just the mourning doves, the least expressive, except vocally, of all the birds we see. But they are the only birds that come to our feeders all year round. And they were the first birds I can remember knowing as a child, at least by their voices. They announced their presence here soon after we moved in, before we had even put up the feeders. I woke early one morning and heard them cooing, the *morning* doves, and remembered from so long ago how that sound gently signaled the beginning of day.

How can that soulful voice, I wonder now, emanate from a creature which, in most other respects, seems so stolid? I regularly see the mourning doves, alone of all the birds, sitting under or even on the feeders as if they were roosting for the night, immobile for as long as I have the patience to watch or until, perhaps, a gang of jays appears and rouses them to resume their singularly mechanical pecking at the seed. The jays leave them alone, and every bird at the feeder defers to them, although I have yet to see one make a threatening gesture. Even when they squabble among themselves they seem impassive, perfunctory.

And yet the doves are the most skittish when alarmed. No other bird flies off so frantically when I come out to refill the feeders. Even the suspicious jays watch me from the trees, waiting to return as soon as I've gone inside again. The mourning doves often disappear for the rest of the day. If it's possible to judge on the strength of what we see, I would be tempted to say that the mourning dove is stupid. Partly, I suppose, I am judging by appearances—the tiny look of the head in relation to the full body. For contrast in behavior, there is the chickadee, fluttering around the feeder, calling to me expectantly, so it seems, as I approach with the fresh supply of seed. At the other end of some sort of scale, the mourning dove evidently connects my presence with nothing but danger.

But once we saw a mourning dove served well by this

heightened sense of danger. Without any warning that we detected, we saw a hawk suddenly plummet from the sky toward a motionless, seemingly oblivious dove. In the very instant it seemed certain to us that the hawk must have its prey, we realized that the dove was in flight. At a speed almost too fast for our eyes to follow, it was flying to the woods, pursued by the hawk but eluding it, we thought—so we hoped. For we are greatly attached to the doves, despite their unreasoning fear of us, partly because of their aloof, inscrutable ways. They have a touchingly archaic look, as if long ago they had evolved, just so far and no farther, not to be showy or clever or vivacious, but simply to endure.

We see hawks soaring over our fields and woods all summer long, but only that *once*, in three years, have we seen a hawk's attack. Our hours of watching certain kinds of repetitive behavior are rewarded by a sense of deep familiarity with them, the pleasure of knowing something in intimate detail, but also by the excitement of happening to witness the completely unexpected event we know we may never see again. Just *once* we've seen a Baltimore oriole flashing through the tops of the elms, a pair of mallards startled into flight from the pond, a crow dropping down onto a feeder, only to be challenged and routed by the brazenly proprietary blackbirds. Although they are said to be common in this region, we have seen only one pair of snow buntings, for the few days in our first winter when they appeared at a feeder in the midst of the usual flock of sparrows, two exquisitely pale and delicate little birds we have searched for in vain in the winters since then. When we meet a ruffed grouse in the road it always seems perfectly at home there, even recklessly indifferent to the car's approach; and yet the grouse so rarely let themselves be seen that when we encounter one we stop the car to watch with a feeling of grateful surprise.

It is certainly a pleasure to be surprised in this way, to

be made to consider the inexplicable, to ask oneself unanswerable questions. Why did the barn swallows nest in our barn our first two summers here and fail to return this past summer? The barn was exactly the same, and we saw them still in other barns nearby, enviously, missing their spectacular aerial displays at dawn and dusk. Why would they leave a barn, studded with old nests, that evidently suited them well for so long? And did the killdeer eggs finally hatch, or did some harm come to them? One day they were there and the next gone from that utterly defenseless-looking nest of little stones lying in the upper field. The young leave the nest almost as soon as hatched, so we read, and the parents must be expert at concealment, for we have never come upon another killdeer nest. But seeing those eggs as we did, lying all but on the ground, exposed to the sky, we could only go on wondering about their fate and about the origins of a means of survival that seems so precarious. Whatever we have learned about birds, such questioning reminds us, we still know little enough, and it is a pleasure to be reminded of this. We have hardly begun to make our acquaintance with a world of undreamed-of richness.

If there is one aspect of this world I think I understand clearly now, it is the autonomy of it. To be so struck by this makes me realize that I must, however vaguely, have assumed the opposite, that bird life, like all the rest of nature, perhaps, was a kind of reflection of human life. Now, the least event, the bright glance or shrill call of a single jay, can make me conscious of that separate existence that is almost entirely indifferent to our own. We intrude on the birds' autonomy by feeding them, and they will, for a season, come to rely on the food it pleases us to give them, since we give it faithfully. But I see that even the enthusiastic chickadee comes to our feeders only as a last resort, never so long as the weather is temperate and its wild food is plentiful. And I almost feel that when our summer boarders, the blackbirds, come to our feeders, they are simply being agreeable. Except that I know they are indifferent to us so long as we let them be.

Last May, while we were away for a weekend, a bird began to build a nest in a vent in the ceiling of our porch. Strands of dry grass hanging from this small, round opening alerted us. We thought at once of the fact that it was almost time to put up the screens and install the furniture that make the porch into our summer room. We realized that we could hardly use the room adjoining the porch, our sitting room, without disturbing nesting birds. After a little uneasy discussion, we decided to remove the beginnings of the nest—only the beginnings, after all—and put up the screens.

We learned what kind of bird we were interfering with at dawn the next morning when we were awakened by a soft, insistent tapping. Creeping to the window, we looked out and saw a flicker, tap-tap-tapping with its beak on the roof of the porch, just above the site from which we had excluded it. Every morning for a week we woke to that reproachful sound, and throughout those days, we kept seeing, in the trees nearest the porch, a pair of flickers, and hearing, over and over again, their shrill, uncomprehending cry. As we began to think we *must* take the porch screens down again, the birds disappeared—to make their nest somewhere else, we dearly hoped. I feel remorseful whenever I think of that week, but from it, at the flickers' expense, we learned something once and for all, something almost shockingly unequivocal, about the blind force of the imperatives in the lives of other creatures.

In the largest sense, I know, we are interdependent, the birds and ourselves, and mutually dependent for survival on a single habitat. But in the particular view of the relationship we get here, I am struck by how one-sided it is. We do little or nothing of unquestionable advantage to the birds. On the contrary, our very presence interferes with them. And yet by the hundreds, in dozens of different species, they coexist with us, playing out their ordained biological role to our benefit and providing us endlessly, meanwhile, with interest, amusement, and delight. The last sparrows of a winter afternoon, the first redwing gliding through a summer dawn: from a respectful distance we may regard them as our companions.

Deer and Hunters, Too

ॐ We had expected to have the birds around us in the country, since they are everywhere. While we knew that deer are common all through New England, we hadn't expected that they, too, would become a familiar spectacle and would engage our thoughts in an intimate, sometimes troubling way. It is hard to think of the deer without thinking of the hunters.

The first deer we saw wasn't on our place but in a meadow on the road into town. There it was alone, nibbling the grass, and when we stopped the car it raised its head and looked at us calmly and curiously as we looked at it from the car. It was young, hardly more than a fawn, too young to be afraid. After a minute or two, it went back to its feeding, dismissing us, so we felt, and we drove on, not wanting to spoil an experience that seemed perfectly complete. To have come upon that beautiful, wild young animal so unexpectedly, to have seen it and been seen by it without frightening it, and then to go away: a memory I would do nothing to change.

That was the summer before we moved in. The men working on the house had told us of seeing deer in our fields when they arrived in the morning, and we got our hopes up. But as the weeks went by after our move and we never saw a deer, we began to think that the sights and sounds of our continuous presence had driven them away. And I suppose that perhaps they did need a certain interval to get used to us.

At the beginning of November they came back. We were having our lunch at the table by the glass doors that give onto the view. It was snowing lightly, the first snow of the season, and the view was half obscured by the falling snow and the mist rising from the still-warm earth. We glanced out occasionally to see how the snow and the mist were changing everything, and suddenly, so it seemed, so it almost always seems, there were five deer in the hollow below the front field, feeding on the last windfalls under the apple trees. Because we hadn't seen them come, in that half light and unfamiliar snow, and because we had been waiting in vain for weeks, they seemed like dream figures or like creatures belonging to some ancient myth, animals come to herald or behold or take part in a mystery. They moved slowly, almost ceremoniously, finding the fruit here and there under the trees, and we watched with a kind of solemn joy, as if at the unfolding of a mystery, until at last they slowly walked out of the hollow and disappeared into the woods.

Early the next morning we looked out and saw half a dozen deer. The fields were entirely clear of that light first snow, and the deer were grazing at the far end of the front field as if it had always been their habit to do so. We studied them through the binoculars with a growing sense of excitement—that they should be there, that they should graze so calmly while we watched, that minute after minute should go by without their showing the slightest sign of uneasiness about being in our field. We soon learned how readily startled they can be, but on that particular morning they simply wandered off into the woods after a while, one by one, leaving the field with an empty look it had never had before.

When we saw eight of them at dusk that same day,

grazing right in the middle of the upper field, and then four in the hollow again the following morning, and then ten at that day's end—some in the front and some in the upper fields, but ten, we counted them several times—then we began to believe, but still hardly daring to believe, that these animals were living in our woods and would regularly come to feed in our fields, and we would get to watch them often and at length so long as we didn't disturb them. We had frightened them off the second morning just by closing the fireplace damper with a clang, and several looked up warily that evening at the slight sound we made when we opened an outer door. Silently we shut the door and stayed inside. Wild with excitement but silently, we hurried from room to room that evening to find the best view of that unbelieveable ten, until it was too dark to see them any longer.

In those first days we felt nothing except elation. But not because we lacked reminders of the fact that November is the month when deer are hunted and shot. Long before it begins, the *Sentinel* carries in its news and its advertising columns tidings of the hunting season. The hunting season: less important than Christmas, more important than Easter, almost as wayward a mixture of business, pleasure, and tradition, with the stores full of hunters' gear, and the men arranging to get time off from work, and the restaurants preparing to open before dawn, and even the churches announcing hunters' breakfasts and venison suppers. No one here could be unaware for long of the approach of this season. And we had already told Mr. Burton and Dave Fremont that they could hunt on our place. We had long since decided that we weren't going to post it.

Then we saw the deer and marveled at their presence; one by one we counted them, acknowledging in each one the integrity of a living creature. And yet we didn't decide to forbid the hunters, not then nor since then. Now we have been through three hunting seasons, and in the second, a deer was taken on our place, and some fool put a bullet into our barn door, and another season is just ahead. In the meantime, all during the rest of the year except when the snow is deep, almost every morning and evening we go on seeing the deer and marveling at them and trying to reconcile two opposing states of mind. We couldn't conceive of hunting ourselves, and if somehow we were compelled to, we would do so with a sense of shame and revulsion. And yet we find the hunting that others do not bloodthirsty and brutal but innocent and even honorable.

Just as we had never seen deer roaming free before, so, until we came here, we had never known hunters. Tom Sargent is an honorable man, and so are Mr. Burton and Dave Fremont. They have hunted since they were boys, and their fathers hunted and their grandfathers, generations in an honored tradition. And if it no longer involves the unquestioned necessity of putting food on the table, there is still satisfaction in doing that, the way men used to do it. While we go to the supermarket and accept the handiwork of some unknown butcher in a distant, unseen slaughterhouse. If I should ever give up eating meat, perhaps I would feel free to condemn hunting. We would be glad enough to be able to get some venison ourselves in season, but no one ever seems to have any to spare. Mr. Burton isn't so well off that a hundred pounds of deer in the freezer means nothing to him, and neither is Dave Fremont.

They are not talkative about what it means to them, but I think that most of the hunters we know would give up anything else that they do for their own satisfaction before they gave up hunting. Much as we ourselves dislike the season, if only because we don't feel safe in our own woods and fields, we do like to go out and talk with the hunters we see walking past the house, so eager and alert when they start out, so weary on their return. And yet, we see men who are almost all deeply pleased with their day, even when they didn't so much as glimpse a deer. Some go for years without a kill. We know how elusive the deer must be because we so rarely hear a shot fired, no matter how many hunters we see starting out. But afterwards they will say to us, well, it was a good day to be out in the woods, a fine day, and they smile with pleasure at the recollection of it and with a kind of innocent pleasure in themselves, the hunters.

I don't find it too absurd to see a connection between these men, between Tom and Mr. Burton and Dave Fremont, and the hunters depicted in the most ancient art. They stand fairly within the sanctions of an immemorial pursuit, however much it has changed. Once we saw a girl hunting with her father and brother, and once a young woman out for the walk with her husband. But it is still almost exclusively a masculine pursuit, and why shouldn't it be, although it seems a pity that the women don't have more occasion for getting out into the woods.

Of course, there are the blundering and blustering fools hunting, too, and every year the senseless accidents. We don't like it, fearing to go beyond our lawn, starting whenever the crack of a rifle echoes from the woods. To the surprise and disappointment of the successful hunter, we declined to have a look at the deer killed on our place. It is bad enough to have to see, daily for two weeks, six counting the bow season, the dead deer trussed ignominiously to the hoods of cars and the backs of pickup trucks, so many dead deer. And yet we seem to have taken the part of the hunters, if only by denying the deer such protection as we could offer on our own place.

We uneasily continue to search our consciences, but the hunters are supremely confident. Perhaps it is just this confidence that has overborne our doubts. The hunter believes, no less unshakably than the farmer, that the earth and its creatures were made for man's prudent use. The very existence of this belief, or at least the fact of our own absolute dependence on it, came as a kind of revelation to us here. We bow to it in the farmer, and we have bowed to it in the hunter. If we saw that the deer were being wantonly slaughtered, we would have the clear right and duty to intervene. But that is not what we have seen.

Gil and I have always been free to assume that the earth was made not for our use but for our pleasure. And so, with guilt unresolved, we will go on enjoying the deer. Just about this time last year, when the grapes were ripe, we spent most of a morning watching two young deer, golden brown yearlings as well matched as twins, going after the grapes. The ripe, sweet fruit must have been a novel treat for them. Again and again they returned to the old stone wall where the grapevines lie within easy reach of a deer. They nipped and nibbled at the grapes, but they were playful rather than hungry. They frisked back and forth between the wall and the front field, chased each other through the field into the woods, raced each other back to the grapes, and twice, as we watched from the house, hardly daring to breathe, ran across our front lawn. Time and again when we thought they were gone for good, they rushed back into view and back to the wall, tireless and heedless as children, until the game was over. We waited until we were sure it was over, and then we moved for the first time in almost two hours, stood up, stretched, sighed, and smiled at each other, breaking the spell.

I don't expect to see anything much fairer in nature than those two young animals at play. It is not a sight that is likely to be repeated, although the grapes are ripe again now. I almost prefer that it should remain unique, as an emblematic vision, an epitome, of the loveliness here that is ignorant of what we do or fail to do, the loveliness granted with perfect indifference to us, as if to the most innocent onlookers.

Knowing the Land

 It was necessary to settle the house and enjoyable to start having visitors, but all the while, in our early weeks, we felt we were neglecting an essential project. Despite the hours we'd spent walking with Tom Sargent and by ourselves occasionally later on, we felt we had hardly begun to know our land. *Our* land now, and why had we acquired it if not, at least, to know it?

Time seemed important, as if we faced such a large undertaking there might not be time enough to accomplish it unless we started at once. Our walks with Tom had made the land seem not more compact and accessible but, on the contrary, more expansive and far-flung, wilder. With Tom we were, in a sense, tourists, knowing where we were only when he told us. The map the surveyor had provided, detailing not just the boundaries but also the chief interior landmarks, old roads, brooks, stone walls, cellar holes, seemed to attest to the size and complexity of our domain. We studied that map respectfully, with a not unpleasant sense that we might, literally, be lost without it.

With our first visitors, we merely strolled, out across the front field and perhaps a short way into the woods, or to the top of the upper field and into the woods around the pond. Most visitors, we have found, prefer the gentle stroll, but we were not prepared then, in any case, to march them along. Even when we set for ourselves such a large, visible destination as the pond, we could lose our way. Now, when I think I could reach the pond blindfolded, this seems nearly incredible to me. But the sensation of being lost is unforgettable.

We thought we knew our way to the pond after getting there quite directly once or twice, but several times in those first weeks we missed it by an acre or more. Pressing through the deep woods, looking for the glint of sunlight on water, realizing after a while that we must have come too far, we would turn back finally and, trying to correct our course, sometimes come back out into the upper field still without having glimpsed the pond's bright surface. And often at some point on these walks we didn't know where we were. We knew, of course, that we could go in any direction and, in less than half an hour, see our own or some other house. Of course, there was nothing to fear. But for a few minutes, at least, while we were *lost*, we felt a heightened alertness, an intense awareness of our physical surroundings that was like a prelude to fear but which, with nothing to fear, was exhilarating. I remember feeling supremely alive.

Soon we learned the route to the pond, and how simple it seemed once we knew it. We could stroll along it with visitors or stride along by ourselves, confidently. Animals, even the chipmunks, make paths, evidently preferring the convenience and familiarity of a beaten path. We wanted to know where we were going. And yet the experience of not knowing, of finding our way, was wonderfully enjoyable. And yet with every step we took it was coming to an end.

Almost every afternoon in the closing weeks of fall, whenever we were alone and the weather held, after consulting the surveyor's map, we set out, always with some particular purpose in mind, to see how long and deep the hollow was, to follow the full length of a logging road, to make a circuit of the oldest part of the woods, a true forest of pine and hemlock, and at least roughly we would carry out this purpose, stepping along briskly through the short, cool afternoons, stopping to stare, to be silent and listen, starting off again as the light seemed to fade in the silence, guessing at where we were and where we were going, guessing wrong and getting lost for a few exhilarating minutes and finding the way again, the way around or through or back at last to within sight of the house as the sun went behind the hill and the early twilight of approaching winter began. At the house, we would get out the map again, to try to see just where we had been and how we had gotten there and back, impressing on our minds the beginnings of a path.

I remember very well just where we went on a cool, still, brilliant afternoon in early November. The fields were bare and brown by then but glowing in the sun. Except among the oaks, all the leaves were down, and the woods were suddenly full of light. We walked across the lower field and along our east boundary and into the woods south of the field, aiming for the point, deep in the woods, where the map showed the two brooks that start on our land becoming one. We found this point without much difficulty, and then we followed the single brook to see where it leaves our land, flowing toward the river, toward the ocean. Smiling at the thought of this small brook of ours flowing so far, we stood there a while, because it was early still, or so it seemed in the unfamiliar brightness of the woods. We found our way back to the field with no difficulty and walked back up to the house under a sky so bright and blue it seemed the weather might never change, the season never end.

But the next day the first snow fell, and for the next week it was gray and wet and cold, and then the hunting season began. It began to snow in earnest, and we went away for ten days, and when we got back winter had set in. We looked at our map then to see just how much of it we knew. Most of it, we saw. Certain parts of the land we had only passed through, but we had at least passed through almost all of it. Next spring, or even on our snowshoes during the winter, we would know where we were going. It hadn't taken so long—hardly a season.

Of course, we didn't *know* the land then the way we do now. I see now what a sketchy thing that map is. I could take it and crowd every inch of it with detail surveyors don't include. The old sugarbush where some of the trees are fifteen feet around. We know because we measured them. The high point on the ridge where you can see the town, a picturebook village at that distance. The clearings and springs and great gray stone outcrops in the woods. The places in the woods and fields where particular wild flowers grow. The animal runs and burrows. We have accumulated this kind of intimate knowledge gradually. Every time we go out for a walk we notice something new, and even if we should spend the rest of our lives here there would always be something new to see. The weather is always changing. The land changes every year, every season.

But it's been at least two years since we lost our way, even for a moment. The way to the pond or the sugarbush or the ridge is as fixed in my memory now as the way downstairs from our bedroom. Gil has been clearing not just paths through the woods but trails, wide enough for the Blazer. His network of superhighways, I call it. But he needs to use the Blazer to get firewood, and there's plenty on the ground if you can get to it. And visitors enjoy walking on the trails.

In the midst of all the pleasures of our country life that have deepened, I regret this one that has ended. A sense of wilderness.

Taking Root

Winter

༝ Feeling settled and snug, we faced our first country winter calmly enough. But the first snow that fell in earnest knocked the power out for almost twenty-four hours. It hasn't happened since, but once is enough. I wouldn't say I *dread* winter now. But I feel respectful.

By early November we had completed our first winter preparations. There were few to make, so far as we could learn. Since all the windows in the house are double-glazed, we had only the storm doors to put up. On the turnaround by the house we had staked out the route for the snowplows with six-foot saplings. The oil tank was full, and the cellar held a fair supply of firewood. We bought snow shovels. We already had enough warm clothing, and we had our snow-shoes. The cars were ready. We were ready, more than ready, we thought. It was hard to imagine the plows actually needing those six-foot markers, each tipped with a red reflec-tor, to avoid hitting a wall or tree.

We had been told that the previous winter was un-usually mild, but we thought we had prepared as well as anyone could for the worst that might happen, short of an-other blizzard of '88, perhaps. No one we knew looked forward with pleasure to winter, but no one seemed to have any dire recent memories of winter hardship. I imagined the possibility of our having to trek into town on our snowshoes, but it seemed unlikely, especially after I had my first glimpse of a town snowplow when this massive vehicle came up the road, early in November, to test out the route we'd marked.

And Mr. LeBeau would be using his powerful tractor to clear our driveway. And the four-wheel drive of the Blazer would carry us anywhere. It seemed there was no reason to doubt the evidence that winter had been tamed.

The first two or three snows that came and went were simply a spectacle of change and new beauty. It was still so warm, barely freezing, the day the snow began to fall in earnest, we never thought it would last. But by midafternoon there were several inches of wet, heavy snow on the ground and no sign of its stopping. A little after four, just as it was getting dark, the lights went off—and the pump, the furnace, the stove, all the vital machinery of the house. All but the telephone. We called the power company and were only partly reassured. This exceptionally wet snow was bringing trees and branches down on the lines almost as fast as the crews could make repairs. We lit candles and built up the sitting room fire. And the power came back on a little after six. I cooked dinner, and halfway through it we were in the dark again. For good, so to speak. The snow continued to fall, and the power company declined to make predictions.

We hadn't realized how quickly the water stops running when the pump stops—within minutes. Since the outside temperature still was not much below freezing, it took several hours for the furnace heat to die away. Gil kept fires going in the sitting room and in the Franklin stove in our bedroom, and these rooms never got cold. But it's not the same kind of warmth, not when it depends on one's own unaccustomed watchfulness and effort. In the rest of the house, by midnight, the air was dank and chilled. I wondered how long it took for pipes to freeze.

Gil, at the usual time, got ready for bed, put several blankets on our bed to make up for the uselessness of the electric blanket, and, after trying to persuade me to join him, went to bed. I admired his composure, but unreasoning

111

anxiety kept me from following his example. Huddled in a blanket, still fully dressed, I slept fitfully on the sitting room sofa, waking when Gil came down to feed the fire, waking at the sound of the plow approaching the house. I went to the window to see it, and understood once and for all, peering through the cloud of falling snow, the necessity for the markers. But it was a comforting sight, headlights blazing through the snowy darkness, and the engine's roar a comforting sound.

At breakfast time I melted snow and heated the water on top of the Franklin stove for coffee. It was still snowing, but not hard, and in the middle of the morning it stopped. The temperature was dropping, but the sun came out. We made our first use of our snow shovels. The plow came around again, and Mr. LeBeau appeared to clear the drive. His plant was shut down, along with almost everything else in Whitcomb except the town garage and the hospital. But at noon we learned, in talking with Elizabeth, that the power in town had come back on. Surely that meant ours would soon be on. But the idea of the town, humming away again, was irresistible. We sped to the shopping center on roads thoroughly plowed and sanded, lunched happily on hamburgers, idled around the stores in the midst of crowds that seemed to share our inordinate sense of elation, and returned at last to find our disabled house functioning once more.

So that was all there was to it—nothing, really, nothing except the most minor inconvenience. Except that we had discovered our vulnerability to the weather. We had seen our carefully planned house become little more than a shell, hardly as well equipped for winter survival as the pioneer's cabin. We had experienced city power failures among thousands or millions of people, a social experience, and perceived them as a breakdown in man-made arrangements, as a temporary defect in a system under human control. We were alone in our country house, half a mile from the next house, and cut off from the world if only by our own unfamiliar sense of isolation. Clinging to the notion of responsible authority, I berated the power company to Gil when, by rights, I should have shaken my fist at the sky. We had only to look out to see, or open the door to hear, what the snow was doing to the trees. And little in our experience enabled us to judge the possible duration or severity of the storm.

Being by nature calm and sensible, Gil went to bed as usual during the storm. I didn't expect him to share my vigil. It was reassuring to me that he could go to sleep. But being by nature apprehensive, I tossed and turned on the sofa, feeling helpless, feeling shaken by a sense of misplaced confidence. I had *counted* on the house in a way that seemed to have proved illusory. Apparently, I had left the weather out of account. Suppose the pipes burst. Suppose a fire broke out. Suppose one of us had an accident or sudden illness. I rehearsed such fears, in preference to nameless fears, trying to recover faith, not in the house, but in my own competence and self-reliance.

We have had several short power failures in summer storms since then, but never again for even five minutes in the winter. But we don't doubt that it could happen again, or something more drastic. We have been equipped ever since with battery-powered lamps, transistor radios, Sterno, bottled water, powdered milk, canned meats and vegetables, and always an abundance of firewood. I check over these supplies at the start of winter and try to imagine the possibility of having to rely on them. We have been greatly impressed by the way people here go about their business as usual all winter. Each snowfall is disposed of with practiced efficiency. The schoolchildren hardly ever get a snow holiday. Even if the roads weren't so well tended, we know now from experience that the Blazer moves well through anything but an ice storm. But we don't doubt that the weather may overtake us all again some winter day.

There's a picture in my first album I'm very fond of, a picture taken of me. I'm shoveling the snow from our front walk, in brilliant sunshine, wearing neither boots nor parka. I remember how warm the sun felt as I shoveled that light, fresh snow. I'm smiling in the picture, not for Gil's camera, but from sheer enjoyment of what I was doing on such a day. I see in this picture the image of winter's smiling face, its blue sky, pure air, glittering expanse of snow. It would be hard to exaggerate the pleasure of such days, rare as they are, when the sky is clear, the wind is still, and the snow seems as dry as salt or sand but light and pure as the air and radiant as the sun overhead. We go out on our snowshoes on such days or just walk the half mile to our mailbox. Or shovel snow. I try to keep this image of winter fixed in my mind, against its threatening face.

People here have a way of saying, if we have a few mild winter days, well, we'll pay for it later on. Something childish in this remark always bothers me. As if winter were supposed to be a punishment. As if the weather cared. But it is a punishing season. The town gets a shabby, dispirited look as the weeks go by, with the paint peeling and the pavement cracking and the piles of filthy snow growing, out of the way but never out of sight along the roads. Even the countryside, at winter's end, when the ground is still frozen but bare again, looks bleak and beaten down. While I spurn the notion of winter as penance, I see that it remains, though tamed, an ordeal, by cold, wind, snow, long nights, dark days, by the uncertainty of its risks and rigors and of its very duration. There's nothing much to be done except to wait it out. I wouldn't care to have a day more of it, but I don't mind the waiting, the sense of a kind of long, sober pause, broken by the occasional mild, glittering day, ending, certainly, with joyful spring.

Many people here say they would spend the winter in Florida if they could, and I don't doubt that some of them are sick of it. But I think there is unspoken pride for many in their ability to get through it. Perhaps that's all they mean by that remark about the mild days, that they don't expect to be, in a way don't even wish to be, spared by winter. They don't complain, they go about their business, especially the men, with a fine, casual unconcern. I have been impressed by Gil. He takes our winters seriously enough, but no more. He gets in the wood and keeps the fires going as if he were born to it, reads his book calmly by the fireside on the wildest, coldest nights. I try to take him as my model when I am alone here. For often I choose, even in the winter, not to go to the city when he has to go, and I pride myself now on being able to stay here alone in any weather.

Going Away, Coming Back

After two months in the country, we went away for the first time, to see family at Thanksgiving and do some business in the city. The sun was shining on new snow the day we left, lighting up the landscape with the dazzling light we had barely begun to get used to. Gil stopped the car as we were driving away, and we looked back, stared for a minute or more, in silence. I sighed, or gasped, made some small sound of dismay, and Gil turned to me and I to him, and we smiled at our discovery of the difficulty of going, going off and *leaving* this place.

I thought of it often, perhaps almost hourly, while we were away. We had made every sensible arrangement for its protection, against intruders, against fire and ice. And yet it sometimes seemed, in my most anxious thoughts, pitifully defenseless, helplessly remote and alone, as if our presence assured its safety and our absence had all at once exposed it to every peril. I thought again and again of that lovely last glimpse of it, as if it were to be our last. The very beauty of

115

the image in my mind's eye was disturbing; beauty is too vulnerable, will not be spared. We were busy, we were enjoying ourselves, and all the while, I longed for our return.

Perry LeBeau was to go up to the house every day, to bring the mail, feed the birds, make sure all was well. Each day we heard nothing from him, we could assume that all was well, and the days passed with no word. We had reason to be certain of finding everything just as we had left it, but I remember feeling, and discovering that Gil felt, as we drove the last miles home, deeply uneasy.

I think I will always remember that first homecoming. It was almost dark as we came up our road and over the brow of the hill, but not too dark to see, in a single, avid, exhilarating glance, the house, the barn, the snow-covered fields, the near and distant woods, the near and far hills, and the sky, all just as we had left them, spared in our absence, safe again in our presence, all of it even lovelier than I had dared to imagine it while we were away. With that one glance, our uneasiness vanished. We entered the house as if we'd been out for an hour's walk, saw that, just as reason had told us it would be, everything was in order. But I remember feeling for the rest of that evening, making supper, reading the mail, unpacking, getting ready to go to bed, irresistibly happy. I thought to myself, I'll never go away again, knowing, of course, that I would, meaning only that I understood in a new way how the happiness of my life was bound up with this one particular place.

We have gone away and come back more than a dozen times since then, often enough to make the experience seem something like a ritual, accompanied by certain inescapable states of mind. Why, we ask, must the day of our departure almost always be extravagantly fair? As if we imagine it would be easier to go in dreary weather. That valedictory look: the image we receive must suffice only for a few days, of course, not forever, but we must always take a long last look. The anxious thoughts: they are mostly ritualistic now, a resort to magic, as if we believed that our distant, worried thoughts had proved to have protective powers. The unreasonable, unappeasable tension of the last miles home, and then the almost instantaneous release from it provided by a *single glance*. As if we could see in that glance right through the walls of the house, right into the drawer that holds the silver spoons. Or as if we care nothing about valuable possessions but only that we may find intact a certain prospect of familiar, astonishing beauty.

I don't expect there will ever be a time when we will come and go casually. We are no longer free. We are bound to experience the wrench of parting, the longings and forebodings of separation, the singular reckless elation of returning, while we continue to love this particular place. For it is simply love that detains us here, not convenience or necessity, but love, with its infinite power to disturb happiness or confirm it.

Vermont

It's not being fair to northern Massachusetts, but I always think, as we drive north toward home, that the *country* really begins at the Vermont state line. I know we are a good safe distance then from any proliferating city. But I suppose I am also affected, far more than I realize, by the cult of Vermont, much as I may doubt and disapprove of it.

I have scarcely mentioned Vermont so far, mostly because I believe that what I have to tell about country life isn't true only of Vermont. But there are other reasons, having to do with the cult. I would rather not feed the notion that Vermont has somehow been set aside for all time as an unspoiled green and rural haven. This notion overwhelms

Vermont's own official advertisements for itself and is cherished by wistful, wishful outsiders. I can't think of myself as a Vermonter, and not because of the famous clannishness of the native-born, but I don't consider myself an outsider. I have lived here long enough to believe that Vermonters are just as capable as other people of facing all the risks and temptations of the latter part of the century—and should be allowed to.

Vermonters. The very term smacks of the cult. Vermonters are supposed to be great individualists, but only in certain predictable ways. They are supposed to be wise or at least shrewd, but the rest of us may smile over their homely sayings as we do at their you-can't-get-there-from-here kind of humor. Vermonters are supposed to make syrup and grow apples and cling self-reliantly to a few stony, hilly acres, while the rest of us pursue prosperity and comfort wherever we think we can find them.

Drive out sometime along the back roads and see what clinging to too little for too long can amount to. There is poverty along such roads that may have a pretty setting and may quite likely be more tolerable than it is in the city, but is still shocking, pitiful. But the setting is so green and pretty and hardly spoiled at all by the rusting trailers, makeshift cabins, and decaying farmhouses, and maybe that's just the way self-reliant Vermonters prefer to live. The best thing I can say for the cult is that perhaps it has helped to shield the rural poor of Vermont from the nation's pitying gaze. Most people don't want pity, and how do they put up with so much of it in Appalachia? So, our poor, tucked away in the lovely hills and hollows, can at least enjoy some privacy.

But people born and bred in those hills and hollows have been leaving them for generations. Look at the war memorial in almost any faded little village and see how many men served in the Civil War and how few were left to go off to the

Second World War. The countryside has been emptying out, and filling up again with people living on remittances from the city, people who don't have to try to work the thin soil. People like ourselves.

We greatly enjoy the happenstance that our nearest neighbors still farm in a small way. It's lovely to drive down the road from our place and see cows grazing in the Howletts' and LeBeaus' pastures. Green and rural Vermont. But it's not by farming that any of our neighbors live. It's the work to be had in our reasonably prosperous machinery-making town that supports the farming. You can subsist, maybe, on your lovely hilly acres, or you can sell them to city people, or you can take a job in town. That's all I'm trying to say, really, that there must be jobs. Unless Vermont was actually set aside to be enjoyed by people who have prospered elsewhere.

But, of course, now that *we're* here, I don't want anything to change. Sometimes I think a little anxiously of the fact that Mr. Howlett isn't getting any younger. I can't help wondering what will happen to the Howlett place someday. I want Mr. Howlett to go on forever getting up before dawn to milk his cows. I don't want anyone to sell any land or build any more houses out our way. I don't even care for the fact that Whitcomb is enlarging the sewage treatment plant two miles from us. I mean, wasn't it good enough just the way it's always been? I want everything to stay just the way it is now, and the latter part of the century be damned.

So, I feel safe when we've crossed the Vermont line. But safe from what? From teeming slums and vast industrial wastelands, certainly. There's no danger of that, not in our lifetimes. But what about the prospect of some nice, new, modern-looking factory buildings? Not if we can help it; not out our way, at least. For, of course, we want Vermont to last out our time here just as it is, still green and beautiful.

Betsy Putnam

❧ Early one Saturday morning in December, while we were dressing, I looked out and saw Betsy Putnam making a snowman on our lawn. She finished the head while I watched and gave it a smiling face of twigs and berries. By the time I got outside, she was gone. But the snowman, on the north side of the house, lasted for weeks, presiding benignly over our first winter until the January thaw.

I thanked Betsy for it when I next saw her at Elizabeth's and hoped I had made it plain how pleased I was. I thought I had from the way she smiled, but we were just beginning to understand each other. We were still courting each other then, she with a snowman, I, less eloquently, with my words of praise for it. We remained on rather distant terms that winter, meeting only occasionally and briefly at Elizabeth's or in the road, but I felt quite certain that one day we would know each other better.

And one afternoon in early spring, while I was outside working in the garden, she came pedaling over the brow of the hill on her bicycle and coasted to a stop beside me with a beaming, here-I-am look that marked the true beginning of our friendship, if that is the name for it. We stood outside talking for a while, and then we went in the house and she had some milk and cookies, and we went on talking until she suddenly realized it was supper time at home. The next afternoon after school she was back, and the afternoon after that, but then a week went by and she didn't come. I was disappointed and puzzled, and then I guessed her mother might feel that she was being a nuisance. One morning I put a note in the Putnams' mailbox telling Nancy I would be very glad to see more of Betsy, and that afternoon she reappeared. I was in the house, and she came to the door, and we beamed at each other, beamed at the knowledge that nothing stood in the way of our friendship, if that's the word. And then, because it was a nice afternoon, we went for a walk.

We have gone for many walks since then, in all kinds of weather. She is a fine companion for a walk, lively as a puppy, observant and curious, well supplied with lore. She catches a grass snake, shows it to me, and lets it go. She picks a wild flower or a mushroom and tells me what she knows about it. She notes the various signs of the comings and goings of animals. If we take an unfamiliar way, she is the alert pathfinder.

We have spent countless hours together at the sitting room table on various projects involving the use of paints and felt pens, colored paper, scissors, glue. Or sometimes we play games, sometimes with Gil. Or we go to her house to chat with her mother and sister, study the behavior of the guinea pigs or the hens, discuss the character of the horse or the cow. In the summer, especially when I've had children visiting, she has come with us on expeditions in the car. And, of course, we often meet at her grandmother's.

For a few years, children are so generous in bestowing their interest and affection. I am charmed by this bright, eager, high-spirited child and by our attachment for each other, so fortuitous and yet, evidently, so satisfying to both of us. I don't see how it could exist in the wary, busy city. I suppose it wouldn't exist if I had children of my own or if Betsy had friends of her own age nearby on our road. Circumstance disposed us to enjoy each other's company, but circumstance alone can't account for the mystery of mutual delight.

Our house, the way Gil and I live, our past lives in the distant city and the things I know from that remote and very different life, and talk about sometimes—perhaps all this is in some way attractive to Betsy, apart from the pleasures and interests we share. I can only guess at this, guess at the ways in which I might possibly seem to her a romantic figure. But I know how she seems to me. I know that it is she who most readily tempts me to romanticize country life. Others do, too. Miss Mount, for some of the same reasons, tempts me to see only the marvels and wonders of the country and idealize its possibilities. But Miss Mount is very old, and Betsy's life is almost all possibility still, and my fond fancy would find in her every country virtue and in her life every country blessing.

The great changes are just being prepared. She was almost ten when we met, and now she is almost thirteen. She is still as much at home in nature as any other creature of it. She is quite content to be alone and yet radiant in whatever congenial society circumstance provides. Her family is still the solid center of life, the uncontested source of love and interpreter of law. She is surrounded by beauty. The simplest things amuse her still. She believes in God as trustfully as I believe the sun will rise. But for how much longer?

The other day she came up to show me her new ten-speed bicycle, the longed-for thirteenth birthday present her family had just given her. It is a handsome and responsive machine that will carry her far, to school, to town, to the houses of friends wherever they may live. And she is wonderfully excited by it.

After we had duly admired all its fine points, we said good-by as usual. By now it is a kind of ritual, the way we say good-by. We go on waving as long as we can still see each other, that's all, but it takes a little while. I stood in the drive waving as she pedaled off the other day, and several times, as usual, she glanced back and waved, and she had one hand in the air, waving, as she went over the brow of the hill. It's a loving child's way of saying good-by, and as I watched her go, I wondered how much longer we would continue it.

Perry LeBeau

~~~ The first thing we noticed about Perry LeBeau was the way he worked. While we were still coming and going, we would see the younger LeBeau children playing around their yard, but never Perry. Whenever we saw him he was hoeing the corn, splitting wood, helping his father with the haying or fence mending. He was just thirteen when we moved here and a small boy still, but he worked as soberly and steadily as a man.

So we thought of Perry when we wanted someone to mind our place while we were away. Gil called Mr. LeBeau, and father and son came up to discuss the matter. Or that was the intention. We all tried, or at least Gil and I tried, but no one could get a word from Perry. Until Mr. LeBeau said, not unkindly but commandingly, well, son, do you think you want to do it? And Perry had to reply. Speak up, son, Mr. LeBeau said, and finally Perry nodded his head and murmured *yes*. Just yes, but Mr. LeBeau seemed to be satisfied that he meant it, and so we went on to talk about the exact arrangements. Or rather the three of us did, while Perry sat and listened without saying another word. That was the second thing we noticed about him, his silence. But we thought then that perhaps he was shy with strangers.

Several times that first winter and spring, whenever we had to be away, Perry looked after the house for us. Gil or I would call before a trip, and Perry would say he could come up, yes, he would say, and afterward one of us would call to ask if everything had gone all right, yes, and would he please put his bill in our box, yes. But we couldn't feel we were strangers any longer to this boy who had a key to our house, entered it every day in our absence, and looked after it so well and faithfully that nothing ever went wrong. Especially in those first months, I gladly ascribed to Perry the ability to keep our place safe from harm, and there was no doubt about the care he took with what we asked him to do.

So of course we thought at once of Perry in the spring when we realized we would want a boy to mow the lawn and give me some help with the garden. I called, and he said he could take the job; yes, he said. I suppose we must have talked about the hours and pay, but what I remember is wondering how much longer he would be so silent with me. His silence seemed not unfriendly but wary. We had trusted him with the key to our house. Surely, I thought, when we were working together he would feel at ease with me, and we would talk.

Perry and I have spent three summers and hundreds of hours together since then. We have spaded, hoed, raked, edged, and weeded. We have planted or transplanted, mulched, watered, fed, sprayed, pruned hundreds of different plants in three summers. Last summer we built a wall, gathering up the stones from the old walls in the Blazer, the way Gil and Steve had. Neither of us had ever built a wall before, but there it is, nearly a hundred feet of it, two feet high, running along the edge of the front lawn. We have learned as we've gone along whatever we needed to know. Perry knew about vegetables and farm crops but almost nothing about flowers. I knew even less. We have worked hard together, and he has looked after the garden well and faithfully when I was away. Almost alone he has kept the lawn in its state of near-perfection.

And for three summers I have chatted away to Perry, commented and confided, asked him personal questions, asked his advice, made jokes, thanked and praised him; but still, if he possibly can, he just says yes or no. Or is silent. I have gone on with this often ludicrous, largely fruitless, still determined effort to draw him into ordinary friendly talk, because I can't count him as anything but a friend. Of course

I know it is his way to work so hard at whatever he does and to be silent. But his silence has never seemed unfriendly.

I think I know him a little better than I did three years ago. I know the whole family better, although the LeBeaus remain the least talkative, the wariest, of our neighbors. It is a hard-working, close-knit family, and Perry is the fated eldest child, the sober and steady one. I have extracted certain facts from him. He is taking third-year French, has read *Catcher in the Rye* and some of Robert Frost, plays the trumpet in the school band. He saves most of the money he earns and plans to go to the university. I know he gets high marks in school, not because he tells me but from the honor roll published in the *Sentinel*.

After three years I can get him to smile sometimes and sometimes even to laugh when I'm making my jokes, a quick burst of laughter behind his hand. We have reached such a point just as I am about to lose him. He is sixteen now and a big, tall, strong boy, and next summer he will be working full time for a lumberyard, saving up for the university. He has said he will go on minding our place when we are away, but I don't suppose I'll be seeing him very often any longer.

I've told him how much I'll miss him, and he smiles. I've told him how much it's meant to me, all the work we've done together, and how much I've enjoyed all our summer mornings. I've told him, all too truthfully, that I don't know how I will get along without him, this silent, hard-working boy who is, I hope, my friend.

Gardening

My first effort as a gardener was a failure, with lasting consequences. Timidly asserting myself that first fall, while Mr. Page's men installed the landscaping, I planted a few narcissus bulbs at the far edge of the front lawn. I took sufficient care, or so it seemed at the time, but not one of them came up. I remember all too well how eagerly in the spring I searched the ground for a sign of them, how forlornly at last, when the narcissus in every other garden had bloomed and withered, I abandoned hope.

There were several possible reasons for this failure, and probably it taught me something about planting bulbs, for I've planted hundreds since to good effect. But the experience was instructive in more fundamental ways. Failing made me thoughtful. As the barest beginner, I found myself wondering what gardening was about. One plants and fails or succeeds, and what does it mean and how much does it matter?

Fortunately for my spirits, over the winter I had begun to read, on the assumption that, just as I had learned to cook from books, so I would learn how to garden. I could have learned both from my mother, but thought I had more important things to do. But at least I became familiar with the results of doing both well and with the sort of effort needed. I expected to work hard as a gardener, looked forward to it. And even though I imagined then that I would be occupied chiefly as caretaker of Mr. Page's creation, I was also preparing to do a little planting of my own in the space made available for that purpose by the landscape plan. I pored over two or three encyclopedic garden books that winter and half a dozen nursery catalogues, often feeling daunted by so much expert knowledge, but dreaming a little, dreaming quite modestly, not knowing then of winter's license to dream.

Spring came with no sign of my bulbs but with ample cause to celebrate the season. The spring-flowering shrubs and trees of the landscaping bloomed lavishly, and so did an ancient cherry, spared by the landscaping, and some ruffled, white, sweet-smelling narcissus and regal yellow iris that the Willards must have planted years before. I hadn't noticed them the previous spring, while our building was going on. What a lovely surprise they were, all these hardy, youthful survivors. What did it matter about my bulbs?

But I wasn't in a mood to fail again. For my planting I chose just those annuals and perennials that the books named as all but foolproof and I acquired the plants themselves, well-grown in sizable containers, from Mr. Page's nursery. As if it were yesterday, I remember putting those plants in the ground. I half wish it were possible to feel more than once the devout novice's trembling excitement. While I knew from my reading exactly what I was to do, how different, how strange, how thrilling it seemed actually to be making an opening in the earth and pressing into it the roots of a living plant. I wouldn't care to be so anxious again while doing this simple thing, but would recapture, if only it were possible, the singular happiness I felt at the sight of each zinnia or marigold, daisy or aster, just entrusted by my hands to the earth, to go on living where I had placed it.

Naturally enough, those plants flourished. And what did that tell me? Cautiously still, not forgetting my failure, I took it to mean that most plants of a sufficiently easygoing kind, given a certain amount of care, would thrive or at least survive. Conscious as I was of the small part I had played in getting them started, I could hardly feel that these flourishing plants owed much of their life and strength to me. If they had languished or expired, I suppose at that point I would have blamed myself entirely; but at least I had begun to understand, with a success, something about the limits on the gardener's role. I had guessed that I would forego the gratifications of pride; in return, I have been spared vain self-reproach.

But how enjoyable, how encouraging it was to see those plants taking hold, How much did it matter? It was a fine beginning for that first summer, when a bad one would have been inordinately disheartening. The weather was particularly fine, something I didn't appreciate fully until the following year. The professional landscaping was losing its immaculate look only gradually; its care still seemed simple enough. With diligent Perry at my side, I began to feel ambitious. Planting, it seemed clear to me then, was the supreme experience. While I hesitated to make unauthorized intrusions on the landscaping, I saw how it might be extended. I saw how small it was, a little clearing in the wilderness of the surrounding fields, its boundaries quite arbitrary, determined largely by cost.

Encouraged by every circumstance of this auspicious time, I began breaking new ground. We made a fern garden that summer, Perry and I, heaving the largest ferns we could handle out of the woods, hauling them to the bed we'd prepared at the edge of the lawn. We combed the woods and roadside for the different varieties of fern and made a border for them of potentilla and juniper taken from the fields. Everything lived, still lives, in this favorite, this cherished garden. That was our high accomplishment but not all we did that summer. We began the laborious work of reclaiming the barnyard, evicting rampant weeds from the rich soil, laying out beds, far larger than the fern garden, for planting in the next years. I began to think about building the wall and making beds along it. The possibility of becoming over-extended hadn't yet entered my head.

Every novice gardener should have such a summer, with benign weather, a willing boy, a manageable amount of routine care, an abundance of opportunities to gain a sense of one's own competence and resourcefulness. I was still reading but not so slavishly; there simply wasn't time to do everything by the book. I was working long and hard but finding undreamed of pleasure in it.

Pleasure. What else? I wouldn't bother with gardening

for a moment if it weren't for the pleasure of it, much of which I discovered that first summer. I discovered that I enjoyed the simplest physical tasks of gardening. That I liked the feel and smell of earth. That I was interested by the least phenomena of the infinitely varied life visible in a garden. That whenever I began to work in the garden, I was inexplicably relieved of chronic doubt and felt, instead, a quiet but invincible certainty of the worth of what I was doing.

My pleasures then, and still. And the greatest of all, perhaps, was in store. That winter I turned to the seed and nursery catalogues not as instructional manuals but as what they are, dream books, inspiring and sanctioning sublime visions. Normally, I am a constrained dreamer, rarely venturing far from what I know of reality. With their ideal rendering of remote but real possibility, the catalogues set me free to dream, to create in fantasy an image perhaps not hopelessly remote, since, after all, I was preparing to work toward it, toward an image of spacious, faultless, exquisite achievement. And what a god-like pleasure it is to me still, in the dead of winter, with the last growing season only a memory and the next months away, to sit down with those shamelessly seductive catalogues and a businesslike yellow notepad and lay my plans, the new roses here, the lilies there, an edging of evening primroses, a background of butterfly weed or coreopsis, a new cherry tree or two, a dogwood, a few laurels, and more and more, a lengthening list, with sketches, while in my mind's eye I fashion a precisely detailed image of perfect beauty. Yes, I fully understand the charm of fantasy now. I can make the most beautiful garden bloom in the dead of winter. I don't think I would care to live in a climate without this season for dreams.

Certain kinds of reality caught up with me the second summer. It rained too much, with the inevitable effects. I combatted diseases, insects, weeds, learning to be content with partial or temporary victories, learning when and how to tolerate the forces of disorder, decay, death. Nature commands life to be lived but shows no favoritism. Somewhere in a garden, which is so intimately observed, something is always sickening or dying, if only a leaf or twig. The gardener constantly confronts mortality, can do no more than intervene on the side of life. Even planting is partly a valedictory act: the plant in the ground is at risk. But I went on planting that summer, in a more prosaic spirit, seeing that not everything I planted would prosper or that I might, after all, be disappointed with the looks of some of the choices of my winter dreams.

And I went on planting this summer, when it was too hot and dry. We have filled up the barn beds, Perry and I, built our wall, made and planted the bed on one side of it, made the bed on the other side ready for next summer, and more. I must have some sense of sovereignty over my garden, the real garden, and planting provides it. Now that I am pressing against the limits of time, strength, and even willingness, I feel less imperial, but I think I'll go on planting in a new ground each year, if only for the sake of my dreams.

There was a week early in August when if I stood at a certain distance away from it in the front field and didn't stare too hard at any one part, I thought the garden looked very pretty, not like my winter image, of course, but still, quite presentable. I took up this vantage point several times during the week and felt pleased. But now it's September, and this year's story has been told, and already I have begun to think of next year. Allowed, even required, to live in the future, a gardener always has something to look forward to.

We didn't deliberately plan it that way at the start, but the garden is mine. Gil has all the rest of the place to use essentially as he sees fit, to make his mark where he wishes. I'm thankful for this arrangement. How painful it would be to argue over a garden and how difficult to compromise. Gardening is too demanding to be pursued halfheartedly. I treasure my authority.

The kind of gardening I do isn't taken very seriously around here, and I'm just as glad. Each spring my near neighbors ask me if I'm going to *have a garden*. Meaning vegetables. But I have no interest in giving any more time and thought to food than cooking entails. From their abundance, in any case, our neighbors give us, or sell us when we insist, all the vegetables we can eat. I couldn't possibly improve on John Talcott's cauliflower or Mrs. Howlett's lettuce or squash, and would greatly miss the visiting, the leisurely weather and crop talk, involved in obtaining them. So I'm content that my gardening should be thought of as a kind of amusement for me, nice but not necessary.

The thirty acres of alfalfa the Austins grow on our land show me what a modest effort my garden is. The careless beauty of three seasons of wild flowers mocks my effort. And I'm glad. It was a warning to me, the way I felt when those narcissus failed to grow, almost inconsolable. Since it must be done wholeheartedly, gardening constantly presents the risk of excessive emotion, obsessive involvement. Gardening as a form of insanity, that is! I wish to go on doing it for *pleasure*.

The Austins: Farm People

❧ Roy Austin came over in the spring to plow just as soon as our fields were dry enough to get the tractor onto them. He got the upper field done in pleasant weather, but a cold spring rain was falling the day he started on the front field. We had the sitting room fire going and were staying near it. Hour after hour in the rain, on the open tractor, Roy went around the field. Gil took a thermos of coffee out to him at midday, but he wouldn't stop and come in for some lunch. We watched from the house, shivering a little. When it was time to drive his school bus route, he stopped.

That was a day when we began to understand, perhaps, why so few people still try to farm for a living here. I am not sure I will ever understand just what it is that keeps those few at farming in this cold, stony, hilly part of the world, where, as it happens, there is better-paid work with decent hours for anyone with a farmer's knowledge of machines. It is a commonplace to call it a mystery, but perhaps it truly is beyond reasonable explanation, this attachment to the hardest of lives for a modest kind of living. I have tried to explain it to myself for two and a half years, watching the Austins, Roy and his younger brother Frank, at work.

The Austins, with Joe Blake, the hired man, milk sixty cows and to make ends meet drive the school buses. But land happens to be plentifully available to them beyond their own two hundred acres. There are few farmers but many old farms with fields going begging for use. We could find no one, after Arthur Parsons's death, who would mow our fields for the hay. But the Austins proposed to plant alfalfa if Gil would pay for the seed and fertilizer. Our only other choice, it seemed, was to pay someone to mow and let the hay lie. So, we have thirty acres of excellent alfalfa now that we don't need but the Austins' cows do. The old stone walls in our woods everywhere tell of pasture and crop land abandoned, but at least these thirty acres will be saved, so long as Roy and Frank can use them. And it's probably as close as we will ever get to farming, closer than I ever dreamed of being, knowing the Austins.

Every so often, especially when we have visitors, we go over to their barn to see the afternoon milking. They themselves built, over several years, their spacious, handsome new barn. I like to get there in time to see the cows coming in from the barnyard, filing in by established order of precedence, each one heading for the right stanchion with her name over it, Nellie, Flo, Mabel, Violet, big, ungainly animals filling the barn with their strong animal smell, lumbering into their proper places so that their swollen udders may be relieved of the rich, warm, foamy fluid that we ourselves, once it has been properly presented to us in neat, cool cartons at the supermarket, will drink. There they are, these animals, the improbable source of milk. As often as I have seen them, I am still bemused each time by the thought of our reliance on them and on the calm, practiced, intimate collaboration of animal and man.

It is the calmest place I know, that barn at milking time. The men work quickly, getting the milking machines on and off, but always at a certain steady pace. They will tell the interested visitor as they move up the line something about each animal—Daisy is inclined to kick, Cora is amazingly productive for such an old girl, Helen was the prize-winning heifer of Frank's daughter Jill—the appreciative facts of a long, easy familiarity. Each animal is present only to earn her keep, but there is something like fondness in this commentary that's pleasant to hear. The men talk and laugh occasionally among themselves. They are alert but perfectly at ease. A radio plays popular music loudly, muffling any inadvertent clatter that might make the cows skittish, but even this alien sound comes to seem natural, ordained. The barn cat saunters by, a child wanders in, lingers, and all the while the milk pulses through the clear plastic tubing over our heads, for this is a modern barn, as modern as the Austins can afford to make it, and yet my overwhelming impression when I am there is of a scene essentially unchanged since man and animal first enacted it. And in this deep and curiously comforting sense of timelessness, I am sure I have felt for myself part of the mystery.

If it's a nice day, we often stroll around the farm for a while after the milking. To the old barn to see the calves, past the vegetable garden and the raspberry patch, over to the sheds full of farm machinery, the venerable and the relatively new, and the shop where almost any machine can be repaired, rebuilt, put to some good use. Up to the sugar house, if it's that season, and Roy and Frank are making maple syrup. They made two hundred gallons last spring, just a little side-line, waste not, want not. To our city eyes there is something almost fabulous in all we see, in this living expression of the farmer's fabled self-sufficiency. Never have a garden bigger than your wife can tend, Roy says, a fine joke because it gets to the heart of things. For of course wives and children are not idle; the labor of all is needed to sustain this independent world. *Independence*. You should hear what Frank says about the right to own a gun for a measure of how strictly a man may wish to guard his sense of independence. It's unreasonable, of course, in this day and age, part of the mystery.

There are a few days during the summer, while our fields are being mowed, when there is no mystery at all, when farming, even here, may simply seem to be one of the most enjoyable of occupations. It is a promising time even for us, onlookers, when the Austins' machines begin to fill our old farm lane, the tractor and the mower, the tedder and the rake, the baler and finally the hay wagons, an impressive assembly, ready and waiting. We ourselves have been studying the fields, fancying we can tell when the alfalfa is ready, and we watch the weather, waiting. Then at the dawn of some bright morning we hear the tractor starting up, and we get out of bed to see that the mowing has begun. And then we watch the weather hourly each day, knowing how even a little rain at the wrong time can spoil hay, knowing how even our own spirits will rise when the weather holds right through the baling, and the children come over to ride the wagons, and wagon after wagon goes back to the Austin barn laden with sweet-smelling hay.

The children know what to make of such a day, when the hay is ready to bale and the hot, dry weather is holding. Often there are a dozen or more, Austins and Blakes and neighbor children, boys and girls of all ages. They swarm onto the wagon behind the baler, vying for a part in the work of stacking the bales, making it seem, because there are so many of them, like a game. They ride off to the barn on a laden wagon, waving and cheering from their high perch on the hay. Wherever we look on such a day, we see children making it a holiday. And the tired men, too, are elated at the end, exultant, we see, when we go out to say good-by. Roy or Frank hauls the last wagon away, toots the horn of the truck exultantly as he heads for home. We stand outside in the gathering darkness, in the sudden silence, feeling let down, feeling excluded, as if this marvelously enjoyable day were continuing, over at the Austins', without us.

But often enough it rains, of course, and that's another story, a blow at the time, soon absorbed, put into the long perspective. Roy calls the front field our rain piece, because it so often gets the untimely rain, and he tells us his grandfather had just such a field, a rain piece. If only because the Austins know so much that I know nothing of, I find myself remembering whatever they say. Roy says, deer will wait two hours to enter a field. Frank says, of what I take to be a nice, sunny day, it's a weather breeder. He says, when I think a needed rain is coming, all signs lie in a dry time. Roy happens to come by, on Labor Day, when we have a question about our pears. Labor Day is when you pick those pears, he says. I can't look at a cow in a pasture now without wondering if she has a magnet in her. That is what Frank told me, that a grazing cow may swallow barbed wire, bottle tops, and other bits of metal, and a magnet will hold this junk together safely. But

I may have gotten this wrong, or perhaps he was having a little fun with me. I am as certain as if I'd seen them standing watchfully in the woods until some danger passed that deer will wait two hours to enter a field.

If only because they find their own life so absorbing, the Austins rarely seem interested in most of what interests us from ours. They complain a lot, Roy and Frank, as I notice from reading the newspapers farmers seem to, but they are completely absorbed in their life. They complain about the weather, about costs, prices, taxes, about the government, but never about what a hard life it is, because, so they always make me feel, it simply *is* life, not to be judged in terms that suggest comparison. Roy and Frank are the fourth generation of Austins farming here. They have six children between them, the rising generation. Since they themselves are still in early middle age, the question of succession isn't pressing, but they think about it, and we have talked about it, talked about this or that son or daughter as a likely farmer or farm wife. I can't tell from what they say whether they ever worry that no one will want to carry on. They know, far better than I do, the plain economic reasons why so many around here have quit. But how could they stand to think about the end of this *life*?

Twice a day, every day of the year, those sixty cows are milked. Yes, it's a pleasant thing to go over to the Austin barn every now and then for the afternoon milking. But when I wake in the darkness of a bitter winter morning and think of the men at work in the barn, I think, being free to make comparisons, that it's too hard. Before I go back to sleep, I wonder over it again, trying to justify it, can't *reason* it all out, and go to sleep comforted just by this sense of mystery.

Summer

❧ People here are fond of saying that we don't have a summer at all. It's a favorite joke, half rueful, half prideful, that we have ten months of winter and two of poor skiing, or eleven months of winter and July. But perhaps it's just the New England way of deprecating, being modest about, something as lovely as our summers.

As soon as the snow has finally gone for good, in late March or early April, I like to look down the snowless months ahead and put winter in its place. If it's not too far past the first of April, and if, in my mind, I can keep it from snowing until after Thanksgiving, I can see almost eight months ahead in which, whatever else it is, it isn't winter.

I wouldn't cheat spring out of any of its season, but what about those days late in April when suddenly it's so warm we throw open all the windows and go out in shirt-sleeves? In May, I'm sometimes wearing my parka again to work in the garden, but I am working with an urgent sense of how close it's getting to Memorial Day, not, of course, the official beginning of summer, but the day when, officially, it is warm enough to plant. And if I spend the first part of June sheltering my plants from frost, no matter; the new plants are in the ground and will grow, and the alfalfa is growing, may be ready to cut in June. So who is to say exactly when summer begins?

Take as much of June as spring consents to spare and whatever part of September fall will concede, add on all of July and August, and maybe you can make an honest count of three whole months of summer. The only thing I will grant to the jokes is the way this season seems to hurry by. Winter comes as if for good, spring and fall may linger, but summer rarely lets us forget that its days are numbered. I will shelter my plants in June, but won't try to save them from the first hard frost of September, because then it's over. The blackened zinnias tell me exactly when summer has ended.

Our cool summer nights are justly celebrated, but they hint at the deadline. What we who live here like, I swear, is to be able to complain about the heat. Having lived in far warmer climates, where people simply endure the heat the way they endure the cold here, I am especially struck, perhaps, by the undertone of satisfaction in such complaints. Those precious days when we finally get the chill out of our bones! We celebrate by complaining about our rare hot spells. I remember as exquisitely enjoyable two or three days in our first summer so hot I did almost nothing but lie on the sitting room sofa and read. And there may have been ten such days in this unusually warm past summer, the days when we can mop our brows and sigh as if we felt sorry for ourselves and smile with secret pleasure.

But even without such extreme heat, the sun at noon often is fierce enough to give the first and last hours of the day their singular sweetness. Early in the morning, before I'm dressed, while the air is still cool and the grass glistens with dew, I go out and walk around the garden, and my own familiar garden dazzles me with its pure color, enchants me with its freshness and fragrance. After supper, just before sunset, Gil and I walk out into the fields and woods. The earth, the air, and the light itself are cooling down then, but the fields and woods still glow quietly and gently exhale the warmth of midday. What generous days they are, these rare, prized, perfect summer days that have these beginnings and endings. One such day I take to be the crown of the year.

But then the summer birds begin to go and the crickets start up, and it's a little too cool in the morning to go out in my wrapper and a little too cool after supper to go out without a sweater, and the chilly nights of late August warn that the deadline is near. The last of the hay is cut, and the children go back to school. We have picked the pears on Labor Day. The apples are ripening. But the zinnias are still laden with blooms, as if they didn't know, or as if they did. And, if I'm smart enough or lucky enough, I have bunches and bunches in vases on the last summer afternoon. But if the frost takes me by surprise, never mind. Summer is *over*.

The Animal Question

~&~ In my first album, there is a picture of a baby wood-chuck that I took early in our first summer. From the house I had seen the cunning little creature come out of the barn where, as we now know, a woodchuck raises its young each year. This baby found a large, luscious patch of clover at the edge of the front field and was nibbling too busily to notice my approach from the house. Obligingly, it froze when I was two or three feet away. At the camera's click, it bolted, but I had my picture. There it is in my first album, a bright-eyed ball of fur, full of baby charm, my enemy.

I knew animals, before we moved to the country, as pets and in zoos. I had known them as the lovable figures of childhood storybooks. Nothing of this prepared me to deal dispassionately with the woodchuck, or with any animal whose essential purposes cross my own.

How nice, we thought that first summer, to have wood-chucks in the barn. But early in the second summer, soon after the barn flower beds had been planted, I discovered for myself that the woodchuck is, indeed, from the gardener's view-point, a kind of enemy. Over several mornings most of the new plants by the barn were eaten down to the ground. I remember with astonishment still the rage and rancor I felt at the sight of this devastation.

Gardeners take many harmless measures against woodchucks, most of them, as I have learned, also quite ineffective. Around the barn I have prevailed at last, or for the time being at least, by planting the thorniest of roses. But the enemy hasn't been spared my vengeful spirit. The country attitude toward woodchucks is calmly ruthless, and it has served. Mr. Burton, Tom Sargent, Frank Austin, and other men and boys come up to our place to shoot woodchucks whenever they can, and they know they are welcome. But I recall with complete astonishment how close I came myself to doing deadly harm to the barn woodchucks after they destroyed my planting.

I didn't actually help him set them, if only because I didn't know how, but I did actually stand and watch one evening, out by the barn, while Roy Austin set three steel-toothed woodchuck traps. Gil was away and I was alone. Roy appeared with the traps and proposed to put them out, and I agreed. Roy went home and I went to bed. I slept badly, woke several times, and just before dawn rushed out to the barn and sprang the traps with a long stick. Roy had meant to be friendly, helpful, and was doing something by country standards commonplace and proper. But I felt my complicity was shameful.

So how is it to be, I ask myself, when I'm disgusted with the way I vacillate. I came here, so I thought, with a heart full of fond regard for every furred and feathered species. So that wildlife may safely coexist with us, we have chosen not to have a dog or a cat. And yet we trap the field mice who would winter in the house. And yet I mourn over their cold, still little bodies. And yet I don't feel a moment's pity when Frank or Tom or Mr. Burton tells me he got another woodchuck. And yet when I saw this summer's barn babies, or the last time I watched a woodchuck, far from my garden, ambling at peace through the fields, I felt for this animal, too, the old irresistible tenderness.

It seems to me that someone who grows up in the country learns to sort out the animal question early and clearly. Whether always rightly or not is another matter, but at least there seems to be little or no confusion. Pets are dearly and indulgently loved, but every other beast or bird has its fixed place in the scheme of things. Domestic animals are cared for devotedly, but the gallant old rooster goes into the stewpot at last, and the heifer who always answered to her name becomes, as planned, hamburger. The crows are shot for uprooting the newly sprouted corn. The woodchuck is trapped or shot for raiding the vegetable garden or burrowing in the fields. The deer are hunted. It must be hard at first for the children to understand, but soon they learn. They learn that the earth and its creatures were made for man's prudent use.

It's a question I had never thought would be reopened in my own mind. I thought I knew just what I felt and believed. But living in the country has confused me, perhaps hopelessly. I respect the sensible consistency of the country attitude but am unable to adopt it. But what I thought to be my own now too often seems feeble and foolish, sentimentality giving way to temper. I wish I could work it out for myself, this question of human authority over the rest of creation. Living in the country has made me see that it's a matter of life and death.

Using the Land

☞ Gil has said more than once each summer that the next year he is going to have a vegetable garden, and as soon as his work takes him to the city less often, I expect that he will put one in. He is puzzled by my refusal to have anything to do with growing vegetables. I am interested, and half reluctantly impressed, by the spirit that makes him want to *do*

141

something with more of our land, to improve it and make it productive. I don't think Gil will ever especially enjoy, as I do, the monotonous toil of gardening, grubbing in the dirt. But judging by his other involvements with our land, I am sure he will feel satisfied when he finally has the time for a vegetable garden.

This summer in the mail we received a government questionnaire, part of an agriculture census, asking on page after page for information about our *farm*. A computer mistake, I thought, and threw it out. Two weeks later, another copy arrived with a note insisting rather sternly on our duty to complete and return it. So I sat down and wrote, where it seemed to be appropriate, about the Austins and our thirty acres of alfalfa, and about Clyde Ellis and our five thousand Christmas trees, and about the logging Jim Ryan did last summer. And when, after a considerable time, I had finished, I was smiling over this solemn official recognition of what Gil has already done with our land.

He had the Christmas trees put in even before we moved up here, surprising me. I knew that Clyde Ellis, our local forester, had proposed such a plantation, but didn't know Gil had agreed. One day early in the summer before our move, he took me on a walk in a certain direction, and there they were—five thousand seedlings in long neat rows on seven acres of old pasture. It was a captivating sight, all those infant trees, and is a more imposing one now that most of them are waist high. Clyde looks after them and, in another three or four years, will get them to market. By his reckoning, they will bring a fair return on Gil's outlays on them. It's a nice idea, but I think Gil is getting his money's worth in pleasure right now. He often walks out that way. Instead of old pasture land going back to brush, he sees seven acres of thriving trees. An improvement, a crop.

And the alfalfa is a crop, even though we pay some of

the cost of it and the Austins take it all. I notice that Gil always asks them how many bales came off each field in each mowing. He remembers these figures and compares them from mowing to mowing and, so it seems to me, cares about the yield almost as much as Roy and Frank do. And even though we'd be spending more on seed and fertilizer, he's been after the Austins to take on the rest of our fields. Alfalfa is an improvement, as Roy and Frank like to point out, over the old hay in the fields.

We actually received cash, wads of small bills, for the timber that Jim Ryan cut. Jim would come around every week, after he'd been paid by the mill, with our share. That was another of Clyde Ellis's projects, the logging. He got us together with Jim, marked the trees for cutting, and laid out the routes for the skidder. I had never been so close before to a machine as large as a skidder, a machine with tires that stand higher than my head. But Jim has been running one for years, and Clyde is experienced and conscientious, so I assume that what happened in our woods during the logging was only what was supposed to happen.

Gil went out almost every evening while Jim was at work to see what he had done that day. I went out just once and couldn't bring myself to go back again to the woods that were logged until this summer, a year later. Wherever the skidder went to get the felled trees I still see the aftermath of a hurricane. The stumps aren't so raw now, and the piles of slash are shrinking, but I still am depressed in these woods by their look of wanton devastation. But to Gil and Clyde these are woods that have been properly culled and thinned, woods that have been harvested of mature trees so that the younger ones can grow. Gil reminds me that old trees fall in storms all the time.

I like the appearance of the Christmas tree plantation and enjoy every aspect of our tie with the Austins. I greatly dislike the effects of the logging and hope Gil won't want to do any more of it. But I see that he could never be content, as I would be, just to keep our land for our enjoyment of it, as our wild park. This city man who has always worked with symbols and abstractions turns out to have a strain of the country man's practicality and providence. Considering what we paid for the place, there's no net profit to be had in anything he might do with the land, but that isn't the point. He gladly spends countless hours with his chain saw getting our firewood, because it's there to get. He is the one who sees that we pick the pears and some of the apples. As soon as we decide we can afford it, he plans to put a pond in the hollow. He covets a tractor and looks envyingly at our neighbor's fences. He is still tempted by the idea of animals. He has said he is going to plant potatoes in that vegetable garden, and I expect he will. Potatoes!

If we didn't have such a proper house, I could imagine giving up on my own delightful garden-making and letting the wild flowers and field grasses take over. Just let it be, let nature be, and see what happens. I'll never do it, of course. It's just a frivolous fancy I've never even mentioned to Gil. Even though I can't share it, I'm satisfied, finally that his feeling about our land should prevail. His view of what we should do with this place seems to presuppose a long and serious commitment. Surely, I think, he expects to be here when the Christmas trees are ready to sell. Reconciling myself even to the logging, I reason that he must expect to be around to watch the young trees in the woods grow up. I wonder, doubt, hope. But that's another matter.

Elms

꼬 Feeling as if I were attending a public execution, I stood and watched while the last of our four big elms came down

144

this summer. Someone planted those trees, to make shade for the house, more than a century ago, and we have had to take them all down.

The one that was dead when we first saw the place was felled while we were still in the city. The stump was pulled out and there wasn't a sign of it the next time we got up here. Except for a gap. But three trees remained, and as soon as we noticed, early in our first summer, that they were showing symptoms of the elm disease, we called in the experts to try to save them.

We spent hundreds of dollars on various remedies and treatments, but last summer two more were plainly past help, and Jim Ryan took them down while he was doing the logging. I went into town that day, while he did the cutting, but returned to see those two great trees sprawled along the edge of the front field. A man came with a splitter and in a few hours turned them into firewood. The logs are stacked in the cellar, and almost dry enough now for burning.

So we still had one beautiful old elm, and we spent some more money on it and hoped against hope. Last spring it leafed out in the telltale sickly way, and the leaves began to yellow and wither and fall, and we knew by midsummer that this tree, too, was dying.

Gil arranged with Mr. Burton to take it down, but he was in the city the day it happened. I thought I ought to be on hand, just in case. And it turned out to be rather exciting, for a moment or two, when a little breeze sprang up just as Mr. Burton made the last cuts with his chain saw. The tree was roped to his truck, and the truck was parked in the field with its motor running, ready for him to jump into it and pull in the right direction, away from the house. Even I could tell, as I watched from the porch, that the little breeze was untimely. I thought I could see the tree swaying. But Mr. Burton sprinted with amazing speed for his truck, roared off into the

145

field, and brought the tree down safely in his wake. He was grinning with what I took to be relief when he walked back toward the house, and that was all I felt for a moment, just relief at the thought of what might have happened, but didn't. But there was the tree, lying in the field. That had happened. I wished I hadn't seen it.

There's a kind of a hole now, a big blank space, in the view from the house, but I suppose we won't see it after a while. We got used to the emptiness left by the other three—after a while. Next spring we'll probably plant some maples on the line where the elms stood. I just wish we could have saved even *one* of those four old trees.

Old buildings, blocks of old buildings, come down in the city, and I've hardly noticed. But perhaps now I will.

Time and Mr. Hopkins

❧ Mr. Hopkins, who looks after our mower and Gil's chain saw, more or less, made a visit to New York a few years ago just so he could see what the city was like. The elevator man in his hotel was curious, too. It amuses Mr. Hopkins greatly to recall this man asking him, what do people do up there, what do you do with yourselves up there in the country? We had a good laugh over that, Mr. Hopkins and I. He, evidently, is too busy to devote more than some of the time to his small-engine repair service. And I know how busy Gil and I are, if busy is the word.

One afternoon last fall stays in my mind because it was filled with the kind of contentment we are sometimes capable of feeling here. I was planting spring-flowering bulbs in the rough grass between the old cherry tree and the front field. It took some effort to cut through the sod for a hundred or more bulbs, but the day was perfect for it, and I wasn't in a hurry.

While I planted, I could hear Gil at work. From the woodlot nearest the house, the whine and screech of the chain saw intermittently broke the silence. Since I worry a little whenever he uses that saw, I've learned to welcome the ghastly sound of it, assurance that he's still all right. There's always someone on a fine fall day out cutting wood within earshot of us, and the sound of a chain saw has come to seem arcadian. So it seemed that afternoon—the sound of a country man at work. I knew Gil was enjoying himself, and I was having a fine time, too, wielding my spade, digging and delving, planting—like a country woman.

Both of us, in our different ways, were anticipating seasons to come. We were tying ourselves, with the work of our hands, to the life we expected to live on this place. It was a perfectly beautiful afternoon, and that helped. But what I remember feeling most keenly, as something rare and precious, was a sense of the continuity of time, time as the seamless web, as the ceaseless current. A taste of eternity.

We have time here, or we take time. Even though we're so busy. Mr. Hopkins takes time to go fishing or hunting or, if it's that kind of day, to get in his car and drive halfway up the state to see a man about buying or selling or trading something, leaving a note on his door saying, back after lunch maybe, which we will find when we come for the mower or the saw, and Gil, exasperated but also amused and admiring, will say, another of these bootless country errands, for Mr. Hopkins isn't alone in disposing of his time freely and as he sees fit. His yard is full of incapacitated mowing machines, some of which, I notice, have been there for months. Perhaps their owners simply forgot about them or were so busy they forgot they ever intended to mow the lawn. Or perhaps they spent the money they would have owed Mr. Hopkins on something more interesting and enjoyable than getting the lawn mowed. But we are still intent on keeping after our lawn, and Mr. Hopkins, when we find him in, will get right at our mower and have it fixed in no time, while we stand in his yard chatting with him. I like standing there, looking at all those unused, unusable mowers, while no time at all passes, time we didn't think we had, but took.

Most of the time, of course, most people here still have to live by the clock. Jobs, stores, and schools, the town clerk's office, the movie theater are run on time. We have made no deliberate effort to throw off our own accustomed ways of counting out the hours, something I feel a little self-conscious about when the plumber knocks at the door at seven in the morning and we are still in bed, or a neighbor drops in at seven in the evening and we haven't had our supper yet. Much of Whitcomb still lives by the farmer's clock, but except now and then by the plumber, and by the glory of certain summer mornings, we haven't been prompted to rise when most of our neighbors do, and we read, as before, late into the evening. A good part of what we do all day is scarcely changed, except that Gil goes into the study to work instead of to an office, and I, for several months of the year, go out into the garden. I suppose we would find it hard to idle away our days, even if we were quite free to do so. Though we remain on city time, we too determine by the clock that certain hours should be employed to definite purpose.

Necessity, habit, conscience retain their hold on us. But Mr. Hopkins, perhaps, has transmitted to us something of his free spirit. I like to think of him going down to New York that time, just to see what it was like. I wonder what kind of a note he left on his door. He knows that nothing *terrible* will happen if he doesn't do just what he said he'd do just when he said he'd do it. It wouldn't enter his head to feel exasperated with us if we didn't come for the mower or the saw just when we said we would. If he thought about it at all, I guess he would think we'd simply gotten too busy.

Mr. Hopkins's place is in a pretty little hollow, by a rushing brook, with a nice view of wooded hills all around. And while I've never actually caught him at it, I will bet that he spends a certain amount of his time just standing and looking at that view. He has the considering glance and thoughtful smile of a man who stops to look around. We do it at our place often enough, goodness knows. A visitor may ask, what are you looking at? Perhaps it's an unfamiliar bird or an unexpected animal that we would have missed if we hadn't been looking and would have been sorry to miss, but perhaps we have simply stopped to stare. When I stand and stare at the slope of the front field, it looks to me like the very curve of the earth, and I imagine for a moment that I feel the earth turning. Forgetting how busy we are or ought to be, we gaze at the fields, the woods, the sky, while a moment of eternity passes.

A day when we've done just what we set out to do may satisfy conscience. A day when we've done those things that connect us to the country may be filled with contentment. But I hardly ever ask myself here, in that mood of vain and weary self-reproach, what on earth happened to this day? I like to think that's part of the spirit of Mr. Hopkins, not to look back on each day and try to justify it. As if time required *my* justifications! It is not a spirit of fatalism nor of indifference. Perhaps its most essential element is a state of self-forgetfulness. There is no day in the country so bleak or featureless as to withhold this possibility. Each day has a life of its own which, early or late, we are bound to notice. Even if only for a few moments, we are conscious of nothing else but this life. We are absorbed into the universe.

Alone

❧ Gil has to go to the city two or three times a month, to stay each time for several days. I don't go with him more than once a month, and from May until October, while the garden needs almost daily care, I may not go at all. Because I've done it so often now, I don't even remember what it was like the first time I stayed here alone, in our first spring. I can't remember feeling especially anxious, although I may have spent some uneasy moments, because even now, occasionally, at the end of an evening, I am uneasily aware of being alone.

Every so often I am asked by another woman how I can bear to stay by myself in this house half a mile out of sight of any neighbor. The questioner always seems to imply that, bravely or foolishly, I am doing something risky. But I've thought about the risks, especially at the end of an evening, and find them tolerable. What I would find hard to bear, I usually answer, is to go away any oftener.

Being by nature apprehensive, I suppose I wouldn't stay if this didn't seem to be a safe place. And I mean, of course, not just our own house and land but our neighborhood, our town, and the countryside. A safe place. We read the police statistics in Whitcomb's annual report and see that law enforcement overwhelmingly is concerned with the mishaps and transgressions of motorists. We read in the *Sentinel* of the underage, unnamed local youths caught breaking into the supermarket of a weekend. Or perhaps of a bicycle stolen from a porch or a television set disappearing from an empty house. But we have been struck, as we were while valuable, vulnerable goods remained intact during our construction work, by the fine sense of respect for other people's property that evidently prevails here. We have never missed, so far, so much as a flower from the garden. Of course the Howletts lost half their hens five years ago! Our nearest crime. But Mr. Howlett thinks he knows who did it.

A safe place. Who dares, in these times, to make such a claim? People here say that, in the old days, they never used to lock their doors. But now they do. But in the spirit of the times, not because they have learned to mistrust each other. I take care to lock up each night, whether Gil is here or not, in the consciousness, now inflicted on us all, of the world's random malevolence. It's a small ritual against a slight threat that exists, so I assume, whether or not my husband is here. What defense has he, more than I, against nightmare?

But how I miss him at the height of a winter storm! It's the snow and wind and ice I fear that, in some all but unthinkable circumstances, I may prove unequal to. When the snow falls hour after hour, through the night and on into the morning, when the lights flicker and a loose board on the barn begins to bang, when a little thaw and a sharp freeze turn the road to glass—*then* I'm sorry I stayed behind. Then I wonder why I ever fancied I was capable of staying here alone. But the snow stops, the wind dies down, and if the ice doesn't melt soon, the sand truck is sure to come around. The memory of my fearfulness, like the memory of pain, fades and is all but forgotten.

I don't enjoy taking risks and prefer not to test my limited fortitude. But the occasional tension I find unpleasant seems like a small penalty attached to a general state of heightened, quickened awareness. I talk to Gil in New York, talk to neighbors and see them, go into town and see and talk with people there. But much of the time I am entirely alone, the sole, silent human inhabitant of all creation. Or of that portion of it visible only to me. Perhaps the feeling is godlike. My eye is on the sparrow! I feel that I am unique and then forget that I exist just exactly because everything I see, earth, sky, plants, birds, animals, is other than myself and does not recognize me.

If I didn't care for these sensations, I suppose I would

get a dog, as people often suggest. But I am not a mystic and lack the resources to be any kind of true solitary. I have toyed with a vision of eventually becoming a country eccentric, not, I fear, with the radiance of Miss Mount, just a white-haired old woman muttering to myself, or to the chickadees, as I wander through the woods. But when, in fact, after three or four days alone, I begin to talk to myself, to feel a little *strange*, I see that my capacity for being alone is modest and is sustained all the while by the certainty of Gil's return. It's disappointing to me, in a way. In a way I would like this beautiful, beloved place to be *enough*.

The City

🙈 Days before we go away, I get out my city clothes and study them with care. I don't want to look like a country woman in the city. I want to achieve exactly that degree of smartness that will make me indistinguishable from city women of my age, means, and tastes. It's a guise that takes some effort to prepare each time but eases the rest of the transition. No one shall guess, at least from my appearance, how much I seem to have forgotten, in the country, about city life.

Because it's simpler, though it takes longer, we usually drive when I go down to New York with Gil. Down, I say, as if we descended from great heights instead of a gentle hill-side. But down we go, down the map certainly, five hours southward from Whitcomb, down from the green hills onto the crowded urban plain. It hardly takes an hour for the country to begin to disappear, to fade into the straggling, swelling boundaries of one city or the next. I had forgotten that there were so many people. Excited at first, as we start out, by the unaccustomed smartness of my clothes, by the novelty of the long journey, I feel in the last hour increasingly subdued, silenced. I stare from the car at the growing concentration of human life, see it squeezed ever more densely onto less and less ground, squeezed up into the air, higher and higher as we enter New York, and am silenced, as if by the half-forgotten weight of this dense mass of life, somehow compressed into a single city.

It's a kind of weight I feel myself carrying, so long as our visit lasts, a weight I'm no longer used to—not of numbers alone, but of the infinite multiplication of human possibility. No one could survive in the city, I suppose, except by excluding from consciousness most of the time most of this sense of possibility. But what an effort it takes, I find, on coming from the country. I wear myself out trying to buy some simple thing, a dress, a lamp shade, a birthday present for a child, because I've almost forgotten how to choose from apparently limitless variety. I go into a bookstore, look at a dozen or a hundred books, come out again empty-handed. I wear myself out just by noticing too much. I have almost forgotten how to walk through a crowd without seeing every face, hearing every voice, wondering about each life.

A tree can, in a certain sense, be said to be *meaningless*. It exists, that is, and can be observed without having to be explained, interpreted, justified, understood. I've grown used to looking at trees, fields, the sky, to being with pure being. Perhaps that is just what I think trees and fields can tell me, without meaning to, how to *be*. In the city even a tree loses some of its innocence, seems problematical. This one is growing from a neat, bracketed, ivy-covered square of earth, while the next is bedded in litter and filth. Why? Why is that young man with a briefcase striding down Fifth Avenue; why is that old woman huddled on a park bench? Who are all the people on the bus; and where, if anywhere, is the sky? I wear myself out asking questions that always seem to be irrelevant, looking vainly for meaning.

But, of course, we have nice times in the city—seeing friends, eating in favorite restaurants, going to the ballet, to movies and museums, walking in the park. I don't think I ever quite dared to ask myself, while I assumed I had to live in the city, whether or not I liked it, but, of course, I liked these things, the relatively dependable pleasures, the distractions and consolations. After a few days, when it's nearly time to leave, I almost think I'd like to stay a while. The weight of it all seems lighter, and I can remember that once I scarcely felt it, while I was living here. I can almost imagine living here again. If I had to. And yet I scorn the mindless, heartless notion that no one lives in a city except by necessity.

So then we get back into the car and drive back up to the country. I have already told about our homecoming. The happiness of it. But I feel worn out for a day or two, and preoccupied. Why should it have seemed so hard, so exacting and consuming? The city hasn't changed since we went away. So perhaps the country has changed me. Disarmed me. That is what I think when I put away my city clothes. That they serve as a kind of armor.

Fall

The swallows have gone. The blackbirds and their cronies, the grackles and the cowbirds, have gone. The crows, dozens of them, have begun to conduct their complicated fall maneuvers over the fields, leaders calling out the signals, so it seems, to land and take off again, gather and disperse. The woodchucks are fat and sleek-looking, almost replete. The chipmunks are in a frenzy of last-minute greed.

And it's only September. There's just a touch of scarlet

and gold in the woods. Frost has blackened the zinnias, but the roses haven't stopped blooming, and the pansies are coming into their own again. The lawn needs mowing. But the birds and animals know what time of year it is. I watch them with a little envy of their sure grasp of reality. When winter comes, only a hapless robin or two will be taken by surprise.

When winter comes. I try to ignore its approach by making of fall not just one season, but something closer to three.

There will still be lots of summery days in September, with warm noons and sultry afternoons and maybe even a last thunderstorm or two. The lawn will still need mowing, and a few marigolds will survive the frost, bright memorials to summer's sunshine. The bumble bees are still around, but dozing through the cool mornings. I must be careful whenever I pick a flower not to provoke a sleepy bee.

There is nothing left for anyone to say about the height of fall here, dazzling October. And I think, before it happens, that there is nothing more to feel. It's so familiar, after all, if you've lived for a while, this annual crescendo of color. And yet it retains the power of music, heard again and again, to seem each time like a revelation. I think now, as I see the little touches of scarlet and gold here and there, that it's not going to amount to much this year. But one morning I'll look out and be amazed by the reckless splendor of it. I'll rush out once again to take photographs, as if I think the camera sees more than I can, or as if I hope to make it last.

But it goes. With one heavy rain accompanied by wind late in the month, it will be over. The roads will be empty again of all the people who came to see it. The trees, except for the oaks, will be bare. The last of the wild asters will have bloomed and faded. The fields will be bare and brown. And our quietest time will begin. No one wants to visit us in November. No one cares to feel winter hurrying near. November we can keep to ourselves, almost as a secret. Perhaps you have to live here to know what a beautiful month it is— bare, spare, brown, stripped down, grave, and brave. It is a brave-looking landscape we see, stripped of every tender, vulnerable sign of life, reduced to its stark, essential elements. All that we can see we guess will endure, come through. It's a rather grave time, but very beautiful.

For years after I left school, all the years I lived in the city, I suppose, I went on thinking of fall as the beginning of the year. Everything that sets the pace of city life quickens in the fall. Now I couldn't say exactly when the year begins, unless it's at the winter solstice, when the days begin to lengthen, but I know that it ends in the fall. October's color is the year's departing fanfare, November the stillness afterward. If you have a taste for partings and endings, for looking your last at things and living through ultimate moments, but all safely within imagination, of course, you would like it here in November.

Night

❧ The last thing I do at night is to go outside and fill the nearest bird feeder. It's only a few yards from the house, at the edge of the lawn. I go out around eleven every night in every weather. That feeder could just as well be filled in the early evening, or as soon as the birds have gone to roost, but I would be sorry not to have a last glimpse of the night. Unless there's a bitter wind or hard rain, I stand outside a few minutes and look and listen.

I've seen the moon time and again through all its phases, seen moonlight on snow almost as bright as day, seen the wide sky blazing with stars, seen it black, extinguished. I see, and feel, storms coming and see them going away again.

It's lovely to look up and see a little break in a storm cloud, with the moon behind it, and think the morning may be fair. I stand out there trying to guess the next day's weather, and am often fooled, but like to think I know, at night, what the morning will be like.

Even in the dead of winter, I listen hard. We know from seeing in the morning the fresh tracks in the snow how alive the nights are, even in winter. That tantalizing life of the night! We know it exists from the tracks in snow, the tracks in the soft earth of the flower beds and the sandy surface of the road, but it remains almost invisible. Sometimes I find a raccoon cleaning up the seed beneath the feeder, and it calmly finishes doing this before going on its way, the only night visitor quite willing to be seen.

But I listen. For the least crack of a twig in winter, though probably it's just from the deepening cold. For the first note of the peepers from the pond in the spring, for the resonant summer voices of the frogs. And at this time of year, especially, for the hooting of owls, if that's what that sound is. We have never seen an owl. Perhaps it's a porcupine. They hoot, and are mainly nocturnal. But Gil saw a porcupine walking through the fields one afternoon. Perhaps it is a bear hooting, as some say they do.

Gil has seen a bear! One day this summer he walked just a short way into our north woods and heard and then saw a cub shinnying up a tree. Thinking of the mother, he came back out of the woods. Bears are almost unheard of, if not unheard, around here now, but he saw one. And I saw a fisher this summer, another rarity, so we are told. It hurried across the road in front of the car as I was driving down our hill. Fishers are said to be active day and night. They are said to growl and grunt. I don't think I have ever heard one.

Tonight I'll go out and stare into the darkness, not really expecting to see the fox, but knowing it's out there.

Unless it's miles away by now, or dead. The last time Mr. Burton saw a fox, he shot it. He said it was hanging around his chicken house. With the woodchucks on my conscience, I can't very well blame him, can I. There will always be woodchucks, I might argue, but foxes are rare. But I am only guessing about that. I can't tell from the next day's signs or absence of signs what happened in the darkness. I don't know whom the night belongs to. But not to us.

I'll glance over at the barn before I go in. It always looks a little ghostly at night, or enigmatic. That lovely old barn—what are we doing in its life? I'll turn to see the house, glowing with light, and see that it looks substantial enough, familiar, not a dream. Perhaps through a lighted window I'll see Gil still bent over his book, if he hasn't already gone upstairs. I'm not dreaming. This is where we live. In the country.

Then I'll go inside.